Empathy Takes Action

Empathy Takes Action

An Autistic Therapist on the Radical Work of Connection

AIMEE CLIFF

THE EXPERIMENT

NEW YORK

EMPATHY TAKES ACTION: *An Autistic Therapist on the Radical Work of Connection*
Copyright © 2026 by Aimee Cliff

Hannah Emerson, excerpt from "Another Free Blue Vortex" from *The Kissing of Kissing*. Copyright © 2022 by Hannah Emerson. Reprinted with the permission of The Permissions Company, LLC on behalf of Milkweed Editions, milkweed.org.

All rights reserved. Except for brief passages quoted in newspaper, magazine, radio, television, or online reviews, no portion of this book may be reproduced, distributed, or transmitted in any form or by any means, electronic or mechanical, including photocopying, recording, or information storage or retrieval system, without the prior written permission of the publisher.

The Experiment, LLC | 220 East 23rd Street, Suite 600 | New York, NY 10010-4658
theexperimentpublishing.com

This book contains the opinions and ideas of its author. It is intended to provide helpful and informative material on the subjects addressed in the book. It is sold with the understanding that the author and publisher are not engaged in rendering personal professional services in the book. The author and publisher specifically disclaim all responsibility for any liability, loss, or risk—personal or otherwise—that is incurred as a consequence, directly or indirectly, of the use and application of any of the contents of this book.

THE EXPERIMENT and its colophon are registered trademarks of The Experiment, LLC. Many of the designations used by manufacturers and sellers to distinguish their products are claimed as trademarks. Where those designations appear in this book and The Experiment was aware of a trademark claim, the designations have been capitalized.

The Experiment's books are available at special discounts when purchased in bulk for premiums and sales promotions as well as for fundraising or educational use. For details, contact us at info@theexperimentpublishing.com.

Library of Congress Cataloging-in-Publication Data available upon request

ISBN 979-8-89303-102-7
Ebook ISBN 979-8-89303-103-4

Jacket and text design by Beth Bugler
Jacket image by Song_about_summer/Adobe Stock
Author photograph courtesy of Krishanthi Puwanarajah

Manufactured in the United States of America

First printing March 2026
10 9 8 7 6 5 4 3 2 1

For George

Author's note

Throughout this book, the names and other details of anecdotal stories presented have been changed. When writing about people I've worked with in therapy, the stories are rooted in truth, but I have created composites that are fictionalized and distorted beyond recognition to protect confidentiality.

Contents

Introduction: Born to read minds?   1

1 • **Defining empathy**   23
2 • **Empathy is humble**   57
3 • **Empathy is embodied**   89
4 • **Empathy is amoral**   133
5 • **Empathy is radical**   171
6 • **Empathy is work**   207

Notes   241
Further Reading   259
Acknowledgments   261
About the Author   262

Introduction:
Born to read minds?

What do we mean exactly when we say that someone "lacks empathy"? In the past, I never gave it much thought when I used the phrase casually, as most of us do: to describe someone whose lack of consideration for others was beyond the pale, like, say, the British populist leader Nigel Farage or a best friend's ex-boyfriend. It was a catch-all shorthand for people who were unkind, rude, or callous. The person who "lacked empathy" was always the other—until I was diagnosed as autistic in my late twenties. Suddenly, it was me.

The diagnostic criteria for autism includes difficulties in social communication and interaction. In the past, some experts have asserted that autistic people have these difficulties because they lack the ability to feel or express empathy. Though this hypothesis has been robustly challenged and even outright rejected by some, it still shapes our cultural conception of autism. Today, the United Kingdom's National Health Service (NHS) describes autistic people as finding it "hard to understand how other people think or feel."[1] Renowned autism researcher Dr. Uta Frith has argued that, while "most of us are born to read minds," autistic people are missing a "gadget" in our brains, which she describes as being like a GPS for emotional intelligence.[2] Even the word "autism" is taken from the Greek prefix "aut-," meaning "self." From its inception, our condition has been characterized as self-ism: a total fixation with, and inability to see beyond, ourselves.

Incidentally, around the same time I got my diagnosis, I was at the beginning of the long process of training to become a psychotherapist. I was a volunteer counselor at a crisis helpline, where I offered support and reassurance to people struggling with everything from abuse to disordered eating to suicidal thoughts. I had completed my first year of counseling training, and was in the process of applying for a master's degree that would lead to my qualification. The irony was not lost on me. My spare time was dedicated to the practice and study of empathy—a fact that I struggled to reconcile with my recent diagnosis of a disorder that supposedly made me incapable of it. The self-doubt that already lurked in the shadows of my mind—a common feeling among trainee therapists—intensified. Was I pursuing a profession rooted

Introduction: Born to read minds?

in empathy to compensate for something that I naturally lacked?

Empathy, we're told, is what makes us human. In his 2014 bestseller *Empathy: Why It Matters, and How to Get It*, the popular philosopher Roman Krznaric argues that without the sacred trait of empathy, "Mothers would ignore the hunger cries of newborn babies. Charities fighting child poverty would fold due to lack of donations. Few people would make the effort to help a person in a wheelchair trying to open a shop door. Your friends would yawn with boredom as you told them about your marriage breaking up." In fact, he writes, "The capacity to empathize is one of the greatest hidden talents possessed by almost every human being." Among those who don't have this "hidden talent," Krznaric notes, are psychopaths and people on the autism spectrum. "Together they account for no more than around 2 percent of the general population. The other 98 percent of humanity is born to empathize and wired for social connection."[3]

As of July 2020, there were around 7.8 billion people on the planet. This means that there were roughly 156 million autistic or psychopathic people, meeting the criteria for a clinical diagnosis, if we follow the logic of Krznaric's 2 percent estimation. The actual prevalence of autism globally is unknown, with some studies suggesting that as many as one in four autistic children are undiagnosed—so the real figure may be significantly higher.[4]

Krznaric waves away this 2 percent as an aside. He casts

out those who supposedly lack empathy, as I used to do myself, and implies that they're bad people: people who do not donate to charity, hold doors open for others, nor feed our children. It is hopefully unnecessary to point out that these generalizations don't hold true about hundreds of millions of autistic people. But perhaps even more concerning, to me, is the simplistic fairytale that empathy is something that some of us are "wired" for, and others are not.

This depiction of empathy does us all a disservice. I imagine that, if you're not autistic or otherwise neurodivergent, it feels soothing to hear that, without having to self-reflect, work hard, or cultivate any skills, you're already predisposed to be empathetic—you're "born to read minds," in Frith's words. Meanwhile, those accused of lacking the correct wiring or gadgets are left with the impression that they are something less than human. This is, in itself, a barrier to empathy. It stops us from getting curious about other people's experiences and building relationships with them.

There is a much kinder, more hopeful option. Empathy is not a passive personality trait that you are either born with or not; something you either possess or lack. It is something that all of us can access if we choose to. By expanding the definition of empathy to include everyone, and all our myriad, brilliant, strange expressions of it, we can only deepen our ability to empathize and connect with one another.

Introduction: Born to read minds?

An uncomfortable label

My autism diagnosis didn't come out of nowhere. I had experienced enough tumult, confusion, and rejection in relationships that I had been driven to seek a psychiatric assessment in the first place. In fact, I had fought for the assessment, having faced my fair share of the dismissals and invalidation that autistic women often experience from medical professionals. Still, I wasn't quite prepared for the cognitive dissonance that would fragment me on the day that I received a forty-five-page diagnostic report confirming what, on some level, I already knew.

In floods of tears, I called my partner at the time, who was at work, on his lunch break. I was cross-legged, child-like, on the wide gray sofa in our east London flat.

"I got the report back from the psychologist, and she thinks I am," I managed to say. The word "autistic" haunted our conversation, but never crossed my lips. "Are you surprised?"

I remember him pausing, trying to work out the most diplomatic and gentle response. He opted for: "Yes and no."

That "yes and no" was an innocuous throwaway comment, but it came to define how I related to my diagnosis in the following months. I held the label of "autistic" at arm's length, cautiously, like it was a cat that was trying to scratch me. I didn't tell anyone else about it for months.

After putting so much effort into getting my diagnosis, the last thing I expected was to feel resistant to embracing the label. This was what I wanted, wasn't it? As I read the psychological report about myself, I felt an overwhelming sense of relief—I had at last been given a concrete reason why life had always felt hard-edged, too bright, ill-fitting. There was also profound grief, as I mourned what could have been done differently for my younger self, and a slight sense of alienation from myself as I saw memories of playground rejections and teenage years of headphone-wearing isolation reframed as symptoms. Though I was relieved, I was not immune to the social conditioning that told me that it was wrong to have a disordered mind. I felt, most unexpectedly, the sting of shame.

The quiet but persistent voice of internalized ableism whispered in my ear: *Perhaps the report is wrong.* When I'd first voiced my suspicions to the GP, after all, he had told me, "You can't be autistic—you have friends." I had a boyfriend, with whom I'd picked out the very sofa I sat on. I thought of myself as a kind and caring person; I listened when people spoke; I wanted to understand others. I was a voracious reader of fiction and watcher of soaps and romcoms. Writing these thoughts out now, they make me flinch. I know that none of these characteristics is at odds with being an autistic person. But ableism is a pervasive poison, and it seeps into us all, like smoke or microplastics. No matter how much I wanted the label, a lifetime of absorbing harmful messages about autism could not be easily undone. In the months after my diagnosis, as I kept it a closely guarded secret, I became hyper-aware of the

Introduction: Born to read minds?

sharp dagger of these messages wherever I encountered them.

"The caller was autistic," a helpline counselor at the desk next to mine said matter-of-factly, one day, to a supervisor. "So he couldn't talk about his feelings."

I recoiled, wondering if the counselor would have phrased it that way if she knew that an autistic person sat beside her. My job, like hers, was to talk to people about their feelings.

Not long afterward, I went for dinner with a friend, who relayed the story of a new line manager she was struggling to get along with at work. He was blunt and stony-faced, despite her best efforts to charm him; his tone during a one-on-one meeting had felt so belittling that she'd left on the brink of tears.

In an effort to wrap her mind around the dynamic, my friend mused aloud, "It's like he just doesn't get how to act with other people at all—I think he might be somewhere on the spectrum."

Under the table, I pressed my fingernails into my palm. If I had told her about my own secret diagnosis, would my friend make this blasé connection between being coldly unfeeling and being autistic? My friend, who knew me better than almost anyone else, who had felt the depth and heat of my own feelings—would she put me in that box, too?

Each time I faced an interaction like this, my initial anger would soon curdle into fear. Maybe I *wasn't* any good at talking about feelings. Maybe I was as stony and unsympathetic as the man my friend was talking about—and maybe people spoke about me like this behind my back. My worry was fueled by the impossibility of ever knowing for sure whether others felt connected to me as I did to them. Have you ever considered, for example, whether everybody else in the world sees the same color as you when they see the color "red"? What if your "red" and "blue" are reversed for every other person in the world—how would you know? Similarly, the thought kept me awake at night that I could never truly understand what someone else's sadness feels like. When it came to empathizing, how could I ever be sure that I'm getting it right?

As the months and eventually years went by, I found the courage to share my diagnosis with the people around me. Though I'd built this up in my mind to be a shocking revelation, I found that most friends and family members were fairly unsurprised—not to mention unwavering in their acceptance and compassion. I even began to gain more confidence in sharing my identity with casual acquaintances, which led to heartwarming moments of connection as often as it did stranger responses. (A favorite example: a friend of a friend who, wine-drunk and wide-eyed, simply shook her head with a horrified stare and whispered, "No.") I continued with my training as an openly autistic psychotherapist, and found myself to be far from an anomaly. The therapy profession is, in fact, teeming with neurodivergent practitioners, and conversations

Introduction: Born to read minds?

about neurodiversity are plentiful in psychotherapy spaces in the 2020s.

But that stereotype of the cold, uncaring autistic person continued to follow me around. At the very beginning of my master's degree in psychotherapy, I met with the university's disability team, to discuss what support they could offer me. Following the appointment, the disability advisor sent some "teaching and learning support requirements" to my new tutors, ostensibly to let them know how best to support me in their classroom. They included this summary of my presumed difficulties with empathy: "Students with autistic spectrum condition may appear to have problems with social interaction and understanding, skills which may come more naturally to others ... [including] difficulty putting themselves in 'other people's shoes.'"

I was horrified. Under the guise of "supporting" me, I felt that the university's disability team had done the equivalent of emailing my math teacher on the first day of school to say, "Aimee cannot count." To say that a counseling student will struggle to put themselves in other people's shoes is to undermine everything they're training for. My indignant email back to the disability team, asking them to re-word the guidelines, went unanswered. And so, I entered my studies fiercely determined to prove that I could put myself in other people's shoes as easily as anyone else. But I was always swimming upstream, fighting a narrative that overwhelmingly dominates academia, popular culture, and beyond.

Human computers

In the popular imagination, autistic people are "human computers": impossibly technically gifted, but emotionally stunted. In the TV series *The Good Doctor*, a young autistic doctor named Shaun Murphy is a clinical genius, and a social fool. In the pilot episode, another doctor objects to him being allowed to become a surgical resident, stating to a room full of board members, "A surgeon needs to communicate. Not just information—sympathy. Empathy. Can Dr. Murphy do that?"[5] The question hangs in the air, unanswered; the clear implication is that Dr. Murphy, of course, cannot be expected to empathize with his patients.

CBS's long-running primetime comedy *The Big Bang Theory* (and its spin-off, *Young Sheldon*) provides one of pop culture's most famous depictions of autism. Throughout the ten seasons of the show, socially inept physicist Sheldon Cooper displays a deep lack of understanding and curiosity for the lived experience of others—to put it mildly. At his best friend's wedding, Sheldon gives a speech that begins, "The need to find another human being to share one's life with has always puzzled me. Maybe because I'm so interesting all by myself."[6]

The writers claim that Cooper isn't canonically autistic (in the show, he says vaguely that he was tested as a child and not diagnosed). However, he's frequently read as autistic by viewers, and the connection doesn't seem accidental given the character's rigid love of rules and routine, sensory issues, and blunt demeanor. Some autistic viewers even

Introduction: Born to read minds?

champion him as a positive representation—there are many autistic people, after all, who *do* share his profile, for example, by being more interested in their special interests than social relationships. But Cooper is one in a long line of portrayals of a particular autism trope that we've seen over and over again. The message repeatedly and obsessively given by popular culture is that autistic people cannot care for others. They can be mathematically, scientifically, technically brilliant—but we are never shown that they are loving, warm, or kind.

These broad-brushstroke stereotypes have been established since autism was first defined as a medical condition. Autism was first conceptualized, separately but simultaneously, by the Austrian American psychiatrist Leo Kanner and Austrian doctor Hans Asperger in the 1940s, less than a century ago.* Kanner and Asperger both characterized the young autistic people they studied as aloof and strange. The basis of their studies was a search for the deficit in these people: What was it about them that made interacting with them so difficult for the doctors?

---

* Recent historical research has alleged that Hans Asperger collaborated with the Nazi regime in the course of his work, colluding in the murder of autistic children by the Third Reich. For this reason, the term "Asperger's syndrome," and Asperger's work generally, have been renounced by many autistic people today. I include him here only to note his historical role in our cultural and medical understanding of autism. For more detail about the controversy surrounding Asperger, I recommend reading *Asperger's Children: The Origins of Autism in Nazi Vienna* by Edith Sheffer.

Empathy Takes Action

Writing in 1944, Asperger theorized that "human beings normally live in constant interaction with their environment, and react to it continually. However, 'autists' have severely disturbed and considerably limited interaction. The autist is only himself."[7]

From the very outset of autism's definition in Western medicine, we've been characterized as separate from "human beings" and "normal" behavior. Of course, what goes unspoken in Asperger's assessment of autistic children is the viewpoint of the children themselves. It's impossible to know whether the young people described here actually feel limited; instead, what's clear is that Asperger is the one who is disturbed by observing them.

Similarly, the idea that autistic people cannot empathize is based on external observations of how autistic people behave, rather than the self-reported experiences of autistic people. While autistic people have been characterized as self-contained and antisocial since the 1940s, the specific theory that autism involves a "lack of empathy" was born in the 1980s. Like many millennials in the 2020s, this theory is about due its midlife crisis.

In 1985, a cohort of researchers established the "Theory of Mind" (ToM) model of autism. This model suggests that the dominant, defining characteristic of autism is an inability to understand the minds of other people, or a lack of what's known as "cognitive empathy." Importantly, this is distinct from "affective empathy," which is about having an emotional response to the emotions of others. Cognitive

Introduction: Born to read minds?

empathy is the skill of inferring what another person might be thinking, or simply understanding that their perspective is different from yours.

Dr. Simon Baron-Cohen, one of the researchers behind this idea, went on to spend the next few decades developing the ToM model of autism. In 1995, he published the book *Mindblindness*, the title being his term for autistic people's lack of ToM. In this book, he argues that humans have an innate and universal ability to "read minds." In autistic children, he says, there's a delay in developing this skill of "mindreading" or "mentalizing"; we might learn it eventually, he argues, but not at the rate of what he calls "normal" children.[8]

Eight years later, Baron-Cohen built on this theory even further, with perhaps his most famous idea: the "extreme male brain." In his 2003 book *The Essential Difference*, he argued that men's brains are good at "systemizing," while women's are good at "empathizing." Autism, he argued, was a kind of "extreme male brain." According to this theory, the autistic person is far above average when it comes to understanding and creating systems, but haplessly unable to empathize.

In earlier works, such as *Mindblindness*, Baron-Cohen mostly focuses on autistic people's inability to "read minds," or what he describes as cognitive empathy. In *The Essential Difference*, his definition of empathy becomes more diffuse:

"Empathizing is the drive to identify another person's emotions and thoughts, and to respond to them with an appropriate emotion. Empathizing does not entail just the cold calculation of what someone else thinks and feels.... Empathizing occurs when we feel an appropriate emotional reaction, an emotion triggered by the other person's emotion, and it is done in order to understand another person, to predict their behavior, and to connect or resonate with them emotionally."[9]

This goes beyond "mentalizing," or "mind-reading." It reaches out and touches our wider cultural ideas of empathy: as caring about others, as being sensitive, as correctly identifying emotions, and showing so-called "appropriate" emotional reactions yourself.

Since the 1980s, researchers have continued to look for the defect in autistic brains that would explain our supposed inability to empathize in these ways. It has variously been argued that autism entails a lack of cognitive empathy, affective empathy, or both. It's been hypothesized that we don't have "Theory of Mind," that we have "extreme male brains," and that we have a fault in our brain "wiring." These all remain unproven—and in fact, as we'll see later in this book, widely debunked—theories. The more you search for a concrete reason that autistic people supposedly lack empathy, and even for an objective definition of what "normal" empathy is, the more elusive the answers become.

What is "normal"?

Autism research has largely begun to move on from ideas

Introduction: Born to read minds?

about "mindblindness" in recent years. While these models still hold a lot of sway among some scientists, there has also been a boom of refreshing, exciting scholarship suggesting alternative theories about autism, increasingly being offered up by autistic people themselves. But there is still no one "God theory" that explains how every autistic brain works. There is no single theory that accounts for the fact that for every autistic person who is nonspeaking or minimally speaking, there is another who is hyper-verbal; for every autistic person who hates loud music and crowded dance floors, there is another who seeks them out; for every autistic person who reports experiencing little emotion or empathy, there is another person who is hypersensitive and easily overwhelmed by emotions.

The cold and clinical autistic stereotype has also started to give way to a new stereotype: the overemotional empath. Many autistic people have declared themselves, in recent years, to have what is commonly referred to as "hyper-empathy"—often used to describe experiencing others' emotions so vividly, so porously, that it's debilitating. In a checklist of "female" traits of autism that frequently goes viral online, autistic women are described as being extra sensitive, and "highly empathetic, sometimes to the point of confusion."*[10] At the very furthest end of this empathy spectrum, a wildly popular American podcast named *The*

---

* Though it's often described as "female" autism, these characteristics can be associated with highly masking autistic people of any gender. I recommend reading Devon Price's *Unmasking Autism* for more about this topic.

Telepathy Tapes made the outlandish claim in 2025 that some nonspeaking autistic people are telepathic savants who can, quite literally, read minds.[11]

This narrative about autistic people being even *more* "born to read minds" than neurotypical people strikes me as yet another form of stereotyping. It not only plays into an ableist stereotype of autism as a "superpower," but it further entrenches this idea of empathy as something mechanical: a dial that can be turned up or down, a device that can be plugged or unplugged in your brain.

As a therapist, I've found that you can generally get closer to people if you don't try so hard to categorize them. People don't fit neatly into boxes. The real work of therapy is in the messiness of the in-between. Empathizing often involves embracing ambiguity, contradiction, and the grayest of gray areas. This is why I'm so drawn to the nuances of neurodiversity.

"Neurodiversity" is an idea that emerged from online communities of autistic people in the 1990s.[12] By attaching the prefix "neuro-," meaning "brain," to "diversity," the idea is as simple as it seems: that there is diversity in the brains of human beings. Autism can be seen as a part of this natural diversity, as can many other forms of neurodivergence (that is to say, ways in which your brain might "diverge" from what's considered normal). People considered to be "neurodivergent" include people with ADHD, personality disorders, dyslexia, schizophrenia, mental health problems, and more.

Introduction: Born to read minds?

In the 2010s, the autistic academic Nick Walker developed this idea further by proposing something called "the neurodiversity paradigm." Walker argued for a liberatory shift away from viewing neurodivergent people as disordered (through what he calls "the pathology paradigm"), and instead viewing them as part of the natural spectrum of variation in human brains. The neurodiversity paradigm looks at neurodiversity in the same way as other forms of diversity in society: It suggests that there is no "normal" or "correct" way to be a person, only positions of greater or lesser social power. It is not a disorder to be neurodivergent, Walker argues, any more than it might be a disorder to be queer—but it is a position of marginalization and oppression in our society.[13]

It is important to bear in mind that not being a disorder doesn't mean that autism is not a disability. Being autistic in a neuronormative world is undoubtedly disabling, whether you believe that it is a medical disorder. There are many people who may be more profoundly affected by their neurodivergence than I am—those who can't speak, or who struggle to control their physical movements, for example—who may rely on the medical model of autism to get the support they need, and who choose to understand their struggles as a disorder.

But there is something very freeing about questioning the rigid assumptions of the medical model of autism and other forms of neurodivergence, and embracing the expansiveness of the neurodiversity paradigm. When we start to question what institutions and stereotypes have taught us to believe about groups of people—not only autistic people, but people with personality disorders, schizophrenia, and other forms of neurodivergence that carry the stigma of being a "social disorder" or entailing a "lack of empathy"—then we may find new ways to empathize with these people. We may even find new ways to think about empathy itself.

Reimagining empathy

Empathy is far from an exact science. Despite the certainty suggested by the idea of "mind-reading," there is infinite variation and room for error in the ways you might relate to someone else, and the ways they might respond. I find this exciting. Certainty limits our capacity to dream up new perspectives, which limits empathy itself. So this book is an invitation to broaden our imaginative horizons, and a challenge to our old understanding of empathy. For none of us are born mind-readers. If we accept that "mind-reading" is impossible and empathy is not a given for any of us, we're left with one vital question: How can we all work to understand one another better?

In chapter 1, we'll begin by tracing the linguistic and cultural evolution of empathy, which is often broadly and loosely understood, to define our terms. Though there have been many attempts to codify and classify it, empathy remains an ambiguous concept. To empathize better, we

Introduction: Born to read minds?

have to begin by understanding the meaning of empathy itself.

In chapters 2 and 3, we'll look more closely at the psychology and neuroscience of empathy. Scientists have in the past formulated the concept of empathy by looking for the ways in which autistic people, and other people with psychological or neurological "defects," might be "impaired" in it. By letting go of the psychological framing of empathy as "mind-reading," we can also let go of any assumptions we might make about what goes on in the minds of others. This frees us up to empathize more authentically, with tentative curiosity, and a willingness to be wrong. And, by moving on from the narrative of empathy as a "gadget" in the brain, we can also begin to understand how empathy as a process lives not just in our minds, but in our bodies, too.

In chapter 4, we'll unpack society's moralizing about empathy. Is it necessary to be empathetic to be a good person? A lack of empathy is often blamed for some of society's worst crimes, and people who commit harm are demonized with labels such as "narcissist" and "psychopath." But by being willing to embrace the gray areas of our moral worlds, and to humanize even those we morally disagree with, we can all become more empathetic.

In chapter 5, we'll explore how empathy intersects with power, and why it's necessary to redress power imbalances to empathize. In the unjust world we live in, we all have different amounts of power, according to our race, gender, class, disability, and other identities, and so nothing is politically neutral—including empathy. Those of us with more social power have a duty to disentangle how that power blocks our empathy toward those of us with less. Deeply reflecting on the ways society influences our empathy, rather than denying its impact, can only improve our ability to build community.

Chapter 6 will take a closer look at the work that is required when it comes to building that community and strengthening relationships, drawing on lessons from psychotherapy and beyond. Unlike the cozy story of being "wired for social connection," real empathy is hard work. But it's also the most joyful kind of work there is. Of course, as a therapist, I believe that relationship-building is a key stepping stone to liberation and healing. So, by committing to work on empathy, we make a commitment to build a better world.

Fueled by the fear that I might have some innate flaw that meant I was worse at empathizing than other people, I have dedicated a significant part of my life to learning more about empathy and how to practice it. I wonder: How might things change if we *all* assumed that we were starting from the same novice perspective, and we all strived to improve? Instead of assuming that some of us are naturally gifted mind-readers, and others are not, we might open ourselves up to the endless contradictions, surprises, and gifts of other people. Sometimes, this might feel dissonant and discordant. Stepping outside of our

Introduction: Born to read minds?

comfort zones often does. But being brave enough to take that risk, and to imagine empathy differently, might bring us all closer together.

1

Defining empathy

It's around 9 PM on a weeknight in the counseling room of a national crisis helpline. The room smells like hand sanitizer, and is permeated with the thrum of clacking keyboards, and several people saying "and how does that make you *feel?*" at varying pitches. At my desk, amid the crumbs of a half-eaten Pret a Manger sandwich, I've just said goodbye to a caller. I take off my headset, and walk silently out of the room. I shut myself inside a soundproof booth, meant for debriefs and private conversations. The second I'm sitting inside, I hug my knees to my chest and sob.

The voice of the young man I was just speaking to is still ringing in my ears. He sounded at once so fragile, and so much tougher than he knew. He was working his way through the chaotic debris of a very recent bereavement; on the phone, I listened to him pick up pieces of his scattered consciousness and hold them up to the light, as if to say: *Can you see this, too? Am I making any sense? What does it all mean?* His voice was a tiny tremor, frequently broken by tears.

I had to be the stable, solid one while I shared that space with him. I looked at the fragments he shared with me, and validated him: *Yes, I can see it. You're making sense to me. I don't know what it all means, but I'm here with you.* After the call was over, I fell to pieces, too.

My tears, to some, might be taken as an indicator of empathy. We often see "empaths" depicted as people quick to cry; people who feel strongly and overtly. But empathy is something far beyond watery eyes. Empathy is not about being overcome with emotion, or about showing emotion in a particular way—it's about communication and connection. This story about me crying after a call doesn't demonstrate what empathy is, but what empathy is often mistaken for—and what it is not.

How we define empathy matters, just as how bell hooks once approached the word "love": "Imagine how much easier it would be for us to learn how to love if we began with a shared definition."[1] Before anything else, we need to grapple with what it is we're talking about when we talk about empathy. To truly be able to empathize with one another, it's essential that we work toward a shared

Defining empathy

understanding of what empathy actually is. In this chapter, we'll look at where the concept first came from, the multifarious ways in which it has evolved, and the five pillars that I believe form the foundation of real empathy.

Contagious tears

As I sit crying in the soundproof booth, a supervisor comes to sit with me, a key-filled lanyard jangling merrily around his neck. He's wearing flip-flops, even though it's bitterly cold outside. Now he's the stable, solid one, and I'm the one permitted to be a mess.

"Has this call triggered something, or reminded you of a difficult memory?" he asks, a line of concern drawn softly through his forehead.

I shake my head. I've never experienced a bereavement like the one this boy had described to me. "I don't know why it's upset me so much," I sigh, "it's just so ... sad."

That word, "sad," feels pathetic. For a moment in that booth, I feel the heaviness, the impossibility, the finality of loss on my chest. My mind rushes through all the years that lie ahead of the boy, and how much courage it will take him to get through them. I imagine a great yawning expanse of grief, and the overwhelm of standing at its verge.

I ask my supervisor if it's okay to finish my shift a little early and go home, and he nods, "Of course."

Helpline counseling can be a frustratingly limited way

of offering support. On social media, memes abound of people mocking the advice they've been given by crisis counselors: "Have you tried going for a walk, or making a cup of tea?" Though it has its own wisdom, this is the kind of platitude that feels practically offensive when you're overwhelmed; like being advised to fight a house fire with a water pistol.

Before training professionally as a psychotherapist, I spent four years volunteering at this helpline. I often felt nervous at the beginning of shifts, conscious of how easily I could accidentally say something that minimized someone's pain. I tried to pick up each call with a blank slate of a mind, ready to fully absorb the experiences and perspective of the person on the other end of the line. I tried to neutralize myself, and make an abundance of space for the person I was listening to.

But I'm a human being, so I didn't always succeed. There were days when my own life loomed so large in my mind that I was too preoccupied to truly engage with what I was being told. There were callers whose experiences I understood only when I reflected on their words much later, and then there were callers I never understood. There were callers whose experiences mirrored my own so closely that I found myself imagining myself in their shoes; their anger, their sadness became my own. I struggled to hear them over the sound of my own memories, blaring like a fire alarm in my ears.

And, like that caller who was picking his way through

Defining empathy

the wreckage of grief, there were the callers who were too much for me at that time. I frequently spoke to people experiencing enormous trauma: mental health issues, abuse, and bereavement. Due to the very nature of crisis helplines, people would often call when they were in the most acute pain of their lives. I sat with them and held them for a while, but I was not enough. No one phone call could be enough. I was just a tired, burnt-out, mildly hungry person, and for half an hour, I did the best I could to hear them.

During my years of volunteering, I came to realize that when the callers' stories continued to affect me long after the calls were over, and when their tears became mine, that wasn't necessarily empathy. Often, it wasn't even really about *them*. After all, I didn't know those people; I had seen only the distorted fragments of themselves that they'd shown me during a half-hour call. We might call this "emotional contagion": a scientific term for when you find yourself crying at someone else's tears, or laughing at their laughter, "catching" emotions from them as you might catch a cold. Some consider emotional contagion to be a crucial part of empathy, but it is not the whole.

Often, when someone becomes as upset as I was in the soundproof booth, it's because something has hit them where they hurt. But if I had sobbed during the call, it would have reduced the space available for the boy to feel his own feelings. That's why I held back my tears until after hanging up: Containing my own emotions to make way for his was part of my expression of empathy. Because when someone else's emotional distress becomes yours, it also, inevitably, becomes about you.

This isn't to say that these contagious tears weren't fueled by a real sense of profound sympathy for the caller. I felt heartbroken on the caller's behalf. I imagined what it might feel like to be in his position, and my emotional response was overwhelming. This is a kind of compassion, of fellow-feeling, of commiseration. It's no bad thing to care about and be moved by the emotions of others. But empathizing is something that goes beyond feeling sorry for someone, or even feeling moved by their emotions—it's a process of relating between two people.

Before reading the rest of this chapter, I'd encourage you to take out a pen and paper, and jot down your own personal definition of empathy. This is not just a pedantic point about linguistics, as you might be surprised by how difficult it is.

Empathy occupies a strangely outsized space in our cultural imagination for a term that is so loosely defined. Most of us are familiar with it and used to hearing it thrown around synonymously with terms like "compassion" or "kindness" in our everyday lexicon. In any given week, I hear news broadcasters speak of "empathy" on current affairs radio while discussing the national outpouring of grief and anger in response to a terrorist attack. I watch a *Married at First Sight* contestant argue that one of her fellow contestants has "no empathy" for the wife of the person she's been flirting with. I spot an advertisement recruiting for a rebranded Metropolitan Police on the London Underground declaring: "Change needs empathy. Change needs you."[2]

Each of these uses of "empathy" makes sense at a glance, but behind them is a concept that's slippery and elusive. Is empathy feeling grief and anger in response to things happening to other people in other countries? Is it considering the feelings of someone else before you flirt with their husband? Or is it attempting to make positive change within an institutionally racist police force? Is empathy involved somewhere in the process of all of these things, or none of them? To understand how empathy has come to mean all of these things at once—and to work toward a shared re-imagination of it—it's necessary to go back to basics.

The origins of empathy

Let's start with the simplest definition of empathy—the one we teach to children. In an appearance on *Sesame Street* with a red puppet named Murray, actor Mark Ruffalo tells the audience that empathy is "when you're able to understand and care about how someone else is feeling." He demonstrates this by explaining how sad he felt when he lost a favorite teddy bear. Murray the puppet lets out a howling sob, saying he can imagine *exactly* how that feels. Mark, comforting a sniffling Murray, exclaims,

"That was empathy!"[3]

Another way you might have heard empathy explained is through the "Golden Rule": "Treat others as you would like to be treated." Idioms like "walking a mile in someone else's shoes" are also commonly used to explain what empathy is. Think of Harper Lee's famous adage, "You never really understand a person until you consider things from his point of view. Until you climb inside of his skin and walk around in it."[4] Each of these familiar sayings suggests that empathy is a kind of teleportation: the act of putting yourself inside the other, or reading their mind. Taking these idiomatic definitions of empathy altogether, it's also clear that empathy is a process with multiple steps: It's about imagining someone else's perspective, feeling what they're feeling (or rather, what you *imagine* they're feeling), and treating them how you would like to be treated (or how you *imagine* they would like to be treated).

Empathy is often defined by what it's not: its cousin, sympathy. Where sympathy is a kind of distanced pity, empathy is thought to be something closer. Academic, author, and public speaker Brené Brown is commonly seen as the modern authority on empathy. In her 2013 talk "The Power of Vulnerability," she defines empathy as "feeling with people." When seeing someone in a deep hole, she says, the empathetic response is to "climb down [and say], 'I know what it's like down here. And you're not alone.'" Meanwhile, sympathy would be peering down into the hole and saying, "'Ooh! It's bad, huh?'"[5] Brown's metaphor is helpful in its illustration of how empathy entails a kind of physical movement; by climbing into the hole with someone, you make a proactive choice to get closer to their reality. You have to take several steps to get there.

But this distinction is mostly lost in our broader cultural depiction of empathy. If we follow the *Sesame Street* logic that empathy is simply "understanding and caring" about what someone else feels, then my bursting into tears at the helpline was a textbook expression of empathy. But what is it about this definition of empathy that separates it from sympathy or compassion?

In fact, the distinction between "sympathy" and "empathy" has existed in the English language for only a little over one hundred years. Many writers and historians point to the works of Scottish philosophers Adam Smith and David Hume in the mid-eighteenth century as the seed of the concept we today call "empathy." Smith and Hume didn't use this word themselves—they still called it "sympathy." Smith's 1759 work *The Theory of Moral Sentiments* explored how humans make moral decisions. He argued that sympathy—the imagining of what another person might be feeling—was a crucial part of that process. So, from its very inception in the English-speaking imagination, empathy has been conceptually tied to questions of who is "good" and who is "bad."

Smith grappled with the limitations of "sympathy." While he wrote at length about the virtue of trying to imagine the experience of someone else, he also wrote movingly about the impossibility of doing so. When we imagine the experiences of others, there is inevitable difference that gets in the way; we imagine not how the other person is feeling, but how *we would feel* in their position. We can never fully see past ourselves; we are always looking out of windows that are fogged up by our own breath. Or, as Smith put it: "Mankind, though naturally sympathetic, never conceive, for what has befallen another, that degree of passion which naturally animates the person principally concerned."[6]

The word "empathy" as we know it today was coined in the early twentieth century, beginning with the German word *Einfühlung*, which literally means "feeling into." This term, conceived by German philosopher Robert Vischer, wasn't about relating to other people at all. It was about relating to artworks, or aesthetic objects, by projecting yourself into them. Vischer also coined two other terms for ways of relating to art: *Zufühlung*, "feeling toward," and *Nachfühlung*, "feeling along."[7] But it was *Einfühlung* that was picked up and popularized by another German philosopher named Theodor Lipps.

Dropping Vischer's primary concern with the idea of projecting yourself into a piece of art, Lipps more broadly defined *Einfühlung* as having an emotional response to art. Have you ever stood in front of a painting that stirred something deep and inexplicable inside you? Have you ever cried while binge-watching *This Is Us*? These could both be considered a kind of *Einfühlung*.

Defining empathy

Lipps later extended the concept to encompass not only how we relate to art but also how we relate to other people. In 1909, psychologist Edward Titchener decided that we needed an English version of this word. He chose "empathy" based on the Greek *empatheia*, which is translated variously as "passion" or "suffering." (Incidentally, in modern Greek, the word means the approximate opposite of its English equivalent, connoting feelings of prejudice or extreme negativity toward someone else.)

Titchener's neologism caught hold, and over the following years, philosophers and psychologists continued to debate and refine ideas of empathy. Around the 1940s, psychologists began to speak of two distinct characterizations of empathy: "cognitive empathy" and "affective empathy."

Cognitive empathy is broadly defined as the mental process of imagining what a situation might be like from another person's perspective (it's also sometimes called "perspective-taking"). Affective empathy, meanwhile, is more of a punch in the gut. This is the kind of empathy that Mark Ruffalo and his puppet friend were talking about: It's a visceral emotional response to the emotions of others.

We're often told that without empathy, the world would be a worse place—and there is an urgent sense that this is an ever-present danger. Back in 2006, then-Senator Barack Obama told graduates in a commencement speech: "There's a lot of talk in this country about the federal deficit. . . . But I think we should talk more about . . . the empathy deficit—the ability to put ourselves in somebody else's shoes; to see the world through those who are different from us—the child who's hungry, the laid-off steelworker, the immigrant woman who's cleaning up your dorm room."[8] Here, Obama positions empathy as the ability to imagine, and have compassion for, people whose life experiences are very different from our own. The failure to do this, he suggests, is the root of all dysfunction in our society. With various scapegoats to blame—such as the COVID-19 pandemic and the rise of social media—liberal-leaning media have continued to warn of the dangers of a less empathetic world throughout the twenty-first century.[9]

Meanwhile in the 2020s, as right-wing and fascist ideology has grown in strength and the rights of marginalized people have come under attack, an empathy backlash has begun. Elon Musk, businessman and former senior adviser to President Donald Trump, has even made the claim that "the fundamental weakness of Western civilization is empathy."[10] In Musk's view, to be empathetic is "suicidal," as it entails sacrificing one's own needs in service of the other.

When empathy is invoked politically, it's frequently used—in one way or another—to reiterate an "us versus them" stance. We are either urged to extend our empathy to "them," or to revoke it. Whether we choose to empathize or not has ramifications for the assumed "us": the privileged, protected, peaceful ones. When Obama encourages his listener to consider the "laid-off steelworker, the immigrant woman who's cleaning up your dorm room," he speaks to someone with presumed socioeconomic privilege, encouraging them to have compassion for those less well-off than themselves. When Musk calls such empathy "suicidal," he speaks to those who wish to protect their privileges by denying them to others. As such, empathy becomes a top-down virtue of the middle classes—something that deepens the divides between us, rather than bringing us closer.

This is not empathy as I recognize it. Empathy is less of a virtue that we might choose to extend to others, and more a mutual process of connecting with one another—not reaching across an "us versus them" divide, but coming together in a collective "us." Rather than "reading minds," making the leap from one brain to another, it's a process of collaborating to create a shared emotional space. Few have given more thought to how we enter this collaboration than therapists.

Empathy in psychotherapy

In any counseling training course, you will likely be asked what empathy means on your very first day. Though it's a core concept of our profession, every counseling student—and, for that matter, tutor—you encounter is likely to give a slightly different answer. In the process of writing this book, I interviewed and spoke with many other counselors about their own personal definitions of empathy. More than once, the conversation spiraled into an existential headache, usually ending with one or the other of us wringing our hands and exclaiming, "Christ, I don't even know what empathy *is*!"

Our field wasn't always convinced that empathy was in fact necessary for therapy. When Freud first outlined the principles of psychoanalysis in the late nineteenth and early twentieth century, he famously encouraged analysts to think of themselves as being akin to surgeons. The surgeon, Freud wrote, "puts aside all his feelings, even his human sympathy, and concentrates his mental forces on the single aim of performing the operation as skillfully as possible."[11] But as the twentieth century went on, psychoanalysts began to see the value of not just peering at clients from a medical distance, but attempting to build empathetic understanding with them. Nevertheless, the therapy world is vast, and not all practitioners prioritize empathy. Fritz Perls, the German psychiatrist who founded the Gestalt method of therapy, believed that empathizing ran the risk of becoming enmeshed with your client, and so Gestalt therapists aim primarily to build "good contact": a functioning relationship between two separate individuals. But generally, you'd be hard-pressed to find a therapist working in the 2020s who does not see empathy as a core component of successful counseling. This is largely thanks to the American psychologist Carl Rogers, whose work throughout the 1940s and beyond laid the foundations of all talking therapy as we know it today.

Rogers founded the "person-centered" approach, a style of talking therapy in which the client is seen as the expert on their own life, who leads the direction of the therapy. Today, his work informs not only counselors who work in a purely person-centered way, but counselors of all stripes. Along with "congruence" (also known as authenticity) and "unconditional positive regard" (also known as acceptance), Rogers's big idea was that empathy was one of the three "core conditions" needed for therapy to work.

Rogers evolved his own personal definition of empathy throughout his lifetime. In 1961, he wrote that empathic understanding is the ability to sit with a client and "see his private world through his eyes."[12] Famously, he emphasized that empathy was about experiencing the inner world and emotions of someone else "as if" you were them, but without ever losing that "as if" quality. It was important to Rogers that the therapist shouldn't identify with their client so much that they lose a sense of the boundaries around themself.

Later, in the 1970s, Rogers expanded this concept of empathy in a paper titled *Empathic: An Unappreciated Way of Being*. Here, he argued:

> "I believe [empathy] to be a process, rather than a state.... It means temporarily living in his/her life, moving about in it delicately without making

judgments. . . . It includes communicating your sensings of his/her world as you look with fresh and unfrightened eyes at elements of which the individual is fearful. It means frequently checking with him/her as to the accuracy of your sensings, and being guided by the responses you receive. You are a confident companion to the person in his/her inner world."[13]

Rogers's description of empathy is active and multifaceted. It sees empathy not as an innate, unconscious reflex, nor as something that we can extend passively or remotely toward others, but as a proactive process of building an alliance so closely with someone that it feels as though you can imaginatively and emotionally walk around their world with them. This understanding of empathy underpins most modern counseling training. A popular person-centered counseling textbook breaks down "empathy" into a four-step process, giving a simplified version of Rogers's outlook:

Being empathic is:
1. Listening sensitively.
2. Trying to make sense of what you hear.
3. Understanding the other person in their own terms.
4. Checking to see if you've got the meaning right with all its subtleties.[14]

Defining empathy

It makes sense to me that any definition of empathy should necessarily have multiple steps. Practicing empathy, in my experience, is a conscious effort. It involves not only listening to another person, but also making sense of what they share, and most importantly, checking that sense-making with them. This checking is a vital part of the process: To assume you understood the other person's meaning would be to project your own experiences and worldview on to them.

While building my own definition of empathy, I sought out other experienced psychotherapists, to hear about their ways of empathizing in practice. Max Marnau is a psychotherapist based in southeastern Scotland, founder of an international online collective of autistic therapists, and editor of the book *On Being an Autistic Therapist*. She tells me over Zoom one afternoon, as her cat's tail waves in her face, that Rogers's description of empathy as being a "confident companion" in the client's "inner world" can't be improved on. Max felt that reading Rogers for the first time was like finding her tribe. "For me, empathy is not what *I* feel. It's what I see in the client's world."

In her sessions, she believes this kind of empathy comes to life when she is immersed so fully in her clients' worldview that she can sense how her client feels before they can even quite voice it themselves. "Quite often, I can voice meanings in the client's experience of which the client is scarcely aware," she says. "That's often when we start to express things figuratively." She describes a recent session in which she and a client spoke mostly about a painting hanging in the room, of a jetty going out to sea. They discussed whether the client felt she was sitting on the jetty, or in the sea itself. "That felt about as close to pure empathy as you can get. Because we were both in that picture."

Max, who is autistic, says that she thinks in pictures. "Words like 'depression'..." she exhales, and waves a hand. "That doesn't mean anything to me, because it's a social construct. How do you actually feel? 'I feel as if my surfboard has just turned over, and I've been chucked into the sea, and I can't breathe.' Right, *that's* telling me something." As described by Rogers, this kind of empathizing is like a creative collaboration. The client opens up their world to the therapist, and the therapist makes every effort to dive in, exploring with total acceptance and warm curiosity.

For any psychotherapist, there is an undeniably bodily, instinctive element to the practice of empathy and building a good relationship. When I speak with other psychotherapists about what they feel in the therapy room, it's common to hear phrases like, "I felt a tension in my stomach," or "I had a prickling sensation in the palms of my hands," as they try to describe the physical connection that pulled them toward their client. This is a contradiction at the heart of psychotherapeutic empathy: As much as it is a multistep, conscious process, it is also a felt sense. (We'll explore this embodied experience of empathy in more depth in chapter 3.)

Defining empathy

For Sonny Hallett, training as a counselor taught them not *how* to empathize, but how to trust in their instinctual ability. Sonny is an autistic counselor based in Edinburgh, where they co-founded the Autistic Mutual Aid Society Edinburgh (AMASE). Counseling training helped them to recognize the importance of trusting their gut. "I've always had a tendency to intellectualize and to analyze," they reflect, as we chat one rainy afternoon. Sonny is very gently spoken, taking pauses to consider their words carefully. "In the past, I've tried to understand humans by learning 'the rules,' like many autistic people—things like looking up a book on eye contact." But during training, they began to feel more plugged into their felt sense of empathy. "I realized I actually needed to go with feeling, and maybe think of the analysis later."

For Sonny, it was revelatory to reconnect with a buried intuition that they had been taught to mistrust. "Counseling is a particularly useful space for intuition that doesn't follow social norms," Sonny says. They give an example: Say that you're speaking to someone who has been bereaved, and you sense that, underneath the surface, they're not quite as sad as society might expect them to be. You might even get the feeling that this person is a little relieved about the death. In the counseling room, you're uniquely positioned to be able to gently, honestly reflect that feeling to the person, and see if it resonates with them. But if you were to say to that person at the funeral that they "seem relieved"—well, then you'd be putting your foot in your mouth.

Among the empathy "experts" of psychotherapy—people who have dedicated their lives to the pursuit of empathy—there remains the same diversity of opinions about what empathy truly is. Some argue that it's useful, and some feel it's a distraction; some see it as a merging of the self and other, others see it as a strong connection between two distinct individuals; some feel it in the body, some find it more cerebral, and many experience it as a meeting of those two states.

There are so many different ideas about what empathy entails because it comes down to building relationships between people, and relationships are all necessarily different, because people are so different. With this in mind, even the idea of an "empathy expert" feels like an oxymoron. I've learned so much about empathy from psychotherapy—about how to listen well, to make an effort to understand others without assumptions, and to tune into my bodily sensations and instincts. But I've also learned that empathy isn't something you can study and then simply apply, as you might learn how to drive a car. Empathy is not something you *do to* another person. Therapists are not superior, benevolent superhumans, able to shine their beam of empathy on any person they encounter. Empathy is more collaborative and cooperative than this—it demands the participation of two people. You can empathize with someone only as far as they are willing to let you in, and it can only really be called empathy if it connects with the other person.

Defining empathy

In many cases, the ways that people in caring professions are trained to express empathy are based in normative social ideals about what it means to empathize. We're taught to sit with our legs uncrossed, keeping our body language open, although some might feel more comforted if we sat naturally, or even walked around. We're taught to maintain eye contact with our clients, even though this might make some might feel scrutinized or uncomfortable. We're taught not to share details about ourselves or our own experiences, though some clients might find that doing so makes them feel more deeply connected. Rather than practicing empathy, this teaching prepares us to be *seen* to be empathetic in a professional, socially acceptable sense. As Sonny points out, many therapists find that true empathy in the counseling room comes from following your instincts, and learning to do things your own way, rather than sticking too closely to a script.

There is social power in being seen as an "empathetic" person: someone who cleaves closely to these social norms about what an "empath" looks like. This is usually someone white, female, neurotypical, middle-class—I picture her wearing Birkenstocks and a kaftan, and saying something soothing in her gentle received pronunciation. I'm not far from this stereotype myself, and for a time, at the beginning of my therapy training, I believed on some subconcious level that this was the person I was supposed to become in order to be a proper therapist. But this archetypal image is not what empathy really is. She's just someone who emotes and supports in a normative way. Empathy is not something that is limited to a particular kind of person, nor a select few experts. It's something that any of us can do.

A working definition of empathy

We can all only become better at empathizing by working toward a fuller understanding of what empathy is. From my research and experience, I've developed my own working definition of empathy that rests on five key pillars: Empathy is humble, empathy is embodied, empathy is amoral, empathy is radical, and empathy is work. Each of these pillars is vital to my construction of empathy, and none is something that an individual can be "impaired" in, biologically or psychologically speaking.

Firstly, I believe that empathy doesn't assume. To be empathetic, it is necessary to be humble. When I empathize, I attempt to make myself fully open to someone else's experiences, presuming nothing about them, and allowing them to tell me their own story.

To try to understand another person, you have to start by knowing that you *don't* understand that person. You can't guess anything about their experience, or what it's like to be them. If empathy is not a destination, but a journey being taken, there are bound to be missteps and wrong turns along the way. Empathy recognizes that you can't ever fully see things from another person's point of view, and so you have to constantly check your perspective with them. There are limits to how well you can imagine yourself into someone else's shoes when you're separated by race, cultural differences, gender, neurotype, or ability. Even when you share identities or cultural backgrounds, you still might just not be able to relate to where someone else is coming from. To assume that you understand what is going on in someone else's thoughts—that you can "read their mind"—is the opposite of empathy.

"What I learned in [training] was that we're all getting it wrong, all the time," Sonny tells me from their counseling room in Edinburgh. "Empathy isn't some magic that I'm missing. It's just that I've been told that I'm specifically struggling with it my whole life." Sonny noticed as they practiced counseling skills that all the students, neurotypical and neurodivergent alike, sometimes fumbled in their attempts to empathize with others. Sonny learned, like everyone else taking the course, through trial and error—and realized that that's the only way any of us can ever come to understand one another.

Many autistic people are capable of approaching others with the kind of open-minded humility that empathy necessitates. As Max puts it to me, "We [autistic people] have the immense advantage that we have discovered that we *can't* assume. If we don't understand something, we'll ask." After a brief pause, she laughs drily. "And of course, we ask rather a lot." In this way, being autistic can be a benefit when it comes to practicing empathy, rather than an impairment, as you've learned early on that your assumptions or readings of other people may not always be correct. Neurotypical people, on the other hand, might feel more confident in their belief that they can correctly identify the emotions or thoughts of others. This confidence doesn't necessarily translate to accuracy.

Secondly, I believe that empathy is embodied. It is not cognitive *or* affective—it's simultaneously, inextricably, both. The idea that our bodies are separate from our minds is rooted in the seventeenth-century philosophy of René Descartes. These days, many agree that this "mind–body dualism" is outdated, and there is no such thing as a dividing line between your feelings and your thoughts. This intertwined state of body and mind is best encapsulated by the idea of the "bodymind." This term was coined by the psychologist Ken Dychtwald in the 1970s, and was introduced by theorist Margaret Price to the field of disability studies in 2015. The portmanteau means exactly what it sounds like: a view of the body and mind as one. "According to this approach," writes Price, "because mental and physical processes not only affect each other but also give rise to each other—that is, because they tend to act as one, even though they are conventionally understood as two—it makes more sense to refer to them together, in a single term."[15] This is vital to explaining the disabled experience for many people, because our bodily experiences can so shape our mental worlds, and vice versa. Think of pain, for example: When you are in excruciating pain, your mind is as affected as your screaming body. It is not either a physical experience or mental one; it is both.

The same is true of empathy. The idea that autistic people might be impaired in cognitive empathy, while our affective empathy is intact, does not gel with this idea of the "bodymind." Our mental processes exist within the fabric of our sensations and emotions. If I'm truly attuned to your experience, and working hard to imagine what life is like for you, then I'm likely to also be feeling something along with my imagining. And, while it's true that empathy is all about active communication and checking your understanding, it's also partly a leap of faith. Your gut tells you what the other person may be feeling, and what is happening in your relationship dynamic; communication helps you work out the accuracy of that feeling. To connect with each other, we have to also experience ourselves as a connected whole: mind and body together.

Thirdly, I believe that empathy is amoral. This is perhaps one of the hardest lessons to learn about empathy—that it is not about being a good person, nor is it even an inherently good trait. Whom you choose to empathize with, and how you express it, might have moral implications. But while empathy is often used in our culture as a shorthand for goodness or kindness, it is not inherently virtuous. There are many people who self-identify as feeling little empathy who are not bad people, and many who call themselves "empaths" yet do bad things.

Though empathy has long been conceptually tied to

morality, even the Scottish enlightenment philosopher Adam Smith wrote that it is not the "soft power of humanity" that determines how we act in moments of moral dilemma, but "a stronger power. . . . It is reason, principle, conscience, the inhabitant of the breast, the man within, the great judge and arbiter of our conduct."[16] I have a less binary view than Smith did of the relationship between "reason, principle, conscience" and the "soft" emotional power of empathy—I believe both reason and emotion can be involved in moral decision-making. But I do think that there is power in his assertion that it's "the man within," whatever that means to you, that guides your actions. This could be how you think, the choices you make, your soul, your conscience. This is something that cannot be reduced to empathy alone.

We are usually encouraged to see empathetic people as "good," and those who apparently lack empathy as "bad"—and therefore, ironically, to withhold our empathy from the latter. I believe that empathy is about seeing the humanity in everyone, which means that it's necessary to unshackle it from moral superiority. Empathy isn't judgmental—it is not about being right, being good, or being better than anyone else.

The fourth pillar of empathy is that it is radical: It necessitates tearing down power imbalances. By its very nature, we can't do empathy alone. It is not an individual trait, but a communication between two or more people. For Max, as a person-centered therapist, an important aspect of how much it's possible to empathize with someone is how far they're willing to let her in. Max points to the existential psychiatrist Irvin D. Yalom's famous description of empathy as being "[looking] out the other's window."[17] "But if somebody puts a blind over their window," Max says, "I can't see—I can't get in."

This relational aspect of empathy means that it is influenced not only by both people on each side of an interaction, but also by a whole heap of cultural and social factors that shape that interaction. Empathy can't be divorced from social context. And so, it also can't be separated from power. Who we empathize with, and who we view as empathetic, are questions that are loaded with cultural baggage. Empathizing with those who have less social power than ourselves means offering something more than pity, which just reinforces that hierarchy. It means recognizing our positions, and doing what we can to redistribute power.

In the 1993 essay *Don't Mourn for Us*—a seminal work of the neurodiversity movement—autistic activist Jim Sinclair asked: What if it's not autistic children who struggle to understand others, but actually, *you* not trying hard enough to understand their point of view? Sinclair gives the example of a neurotypical parent trying to relate to their autistic child, believing that there's "no getting through," as the child doesn't respond in socially acceptable ways. But, writes Sinclair:

> That does not mean the child is incapable of relating at all. It only means you're assuming a shared system, a shared understanding of signals and meanings, that the child in fact does not share. It's as if you tried to have an intimate conversation with someone who has no comprehension of your language. Of course the person won't understand what you're talking about, won't respond in the way you expect, and may well find the whole interaction confusing and unpleasant.[18]

Sinclair's description of what it's like for communication to fail between a parent and their autistic child doesn't place blame, for once, on the child. Sinclair instead poses a gentle challenge: what are *you* doing to try and understand the child's worldview? How can the two of you find a common language with which to understand each other? This kind of power-redressing empathy takes effort, which many people who occupy a privileged position in society don't put in for those at the margins.

This brings us to my final pillar of empathy: that it is work. It is rewarding work—work that brings us closer together, work that builds the connections that make life worth living—but work nonetheless. It's not something unconscious, like yawning when someone else in the room yawns. This kind of reflexive instinct is not the same thing as the conscious empathy that allows you to truly understand another person. We all read and react to one another's facial expressions and moods all the time, and there is an instinctive, energetic element to empathy. But just as Carl Rogers describes empathy as *walking* around in someone else's world, and Brené Brown discusses *climbing* down into the hole with someone, I see empathy as something active, always in motion. It's not only mirroring what someone is feeling, but working to understand how they're feeling.

There may be various impairments that get in the way of our ability to enter into this process together. A difference in cultural norms, for example, might make it harder for you to understand what someone is communicating to you: Perhaps what looks like rudeness to you is intimacy to them. Or, if someone has a learning difference or disability that means they communicate differently, there may be more barriers to overcome in the process of building empathy. But that doesn't mean, with enough sensitivity and open-mindedness, that these barriers can't be overcome.

These are the things I feel sure of about empathy: that it comes from a place of humility and curiosity, rather than assumptions; that it is a bodymind experience; that it is nonjudgmental; that it is relational; and that it is a conscious process that requires effort. But empathy itself is something beyond these five steps. It is not as simple as bursting into tears when you hear a sad story, nor is it as clinical as working through an "empathy checklist." Like love, it is about connecting with another human being; in this sense, like love, it requires a kind of communion on a soul level.

Telling anyone that they lack the ability to empathize sets them up only to fail. Teaching someone that their empathy is impaired is teaching them to mistrust their own intuition and to never take a leap of faith in trying to understand another person. It can also become a self-fulfilling prophecy: If someone believes themselves unable to empathize, they may never try to practice empathy with others. On the flip side, it can also lead those who believe themselves to be innately empathetic to be complacent. This idea of empathy as a passive, instinctive trait that you either possess or don't is harmful, because it doesn't encourage anyone—neurodivergent or neurotypical, self-identified empath or not—to put the work into relating to one another.

I like the way that Sonny describes it to me, as something that "we're all getting wrong, all the time." Rather than sounding pessimistic, I find this idea liberating. Empathy starts with recognizing that none of us can read minds, and we all have to make an effort to bridge the gaps between us. When it comes to empathizing with others, there is a delicate balance to strike. We must take a leap of faith, trusting our ability and desire to connect, striving to understand one another even when we fall short.

After all, when Harper Lee writes that we can't understand another person until we walk around inside their skin, isn't she saying that we can't *ever* truly understand another person? We *can't* walk around in someone else's skin and know what it's like to be them; we can only, as Rogers describes, try our best to sense what is happening for them without prejudice, and check the accuracy of our sensing. No one has an innate ability to know what someone else is thinking. It's only through concentrated effort, communication, openness, and a lack of judgment that we can begin to put together a picture.

Empathy is not what makes us human

Empathy is so difficult to define because there's an unsolvable paradox at its heart: The platonic ideal of empathy is impossible. We can't ever experience what it's like to be someone else.

Lately, I've begun to question the commonly repeated adage, "empathy is what makes us human." What really makes us human, I'm starting to believe, is how unknowable we are to each other. It's the most impossible, most tragic, most definitive truth about being a human being: No matter how desperate we might feel, sometimes, to know what someone else is thinking, or to take their pain away from them, we can only ever be ourselves. But, even though we are so categorically alone, even though we cannot ever climb into another's mind, we try, over and over again, to make space within ourselves for each other. We slog, we toil, we graft. Understanding each other is a lifetime of difficult work, and we do it anyway. Isn't that so much more profound than imagining a brain that's wired for easy, automatic empathy?

Our modern concept of empathy has moved far away from the idea of *Einfühlung*, or "feeling into," but at their core, both have an active sense of searching. "Feeling into" other people is so much more complicated than feeling into a work of art, because, unlike artworks, people can also reciprocate and "feel into" you. Unlike artworks, people have rich inner lives, that—despite your most patient, most kind, most empathetic efforts—can never be truly understood by you. Still, the idea of "feeling into" conjures up an image of being in a dark room, arms outstretched, trying to feel your way around; or plunging your hands into a bag of objects, trying to identify them by their shape. Empathy can be this kind of grasping, fumbling search for each other.

An image that encapsulates empathy for me comes from a poem by nonspeaking autistic poet Hannah Emerson, from New York. Her poem "Another Free Blue Vortex" begins:

> Love to float
> in the blue
> of your soul
> yes yes—love
> to swim in
> your thinking yes
> yes—please try

> to give me
> permission to go
> to the swimming
> with you yes[19]

Emerson's vivid imagery captures the intensity of a moment when empathy is present: when you can "swim" in another's thinking, bask in the "blue" of their soul. She also highlights that this state depends on a two-way exchange—"please try / to give me / permission to go / to the swimming." We are always asking for others to let us in, and we can wade into their minds only as deeply as they will let us. We don't know anything about the minds of others until they give us that permission to go swimming.

When I left the helpline crying, I was thinking compassionately of the person I had been counseling, but I don't think that was empathy. What was more important, that day, was the way I interacted with the boy while we were on the call together. I carefully tried not to imagine myself in his shoes, but to listen, *really listen*, to his description of what it was like to be *him* in his shoes. I felt some of the dark weight of his sadness settle in my chest, and tried my best to hold it for him, while feeling hyper-conscious of the superficiality of the comforting words I was able to offer. Despite being a stranger, I attempted to convey that my heart was open to him, and give him a sense of safety. I was human, and there were moments when I fumbled in my effort.

But it was the effort itself—my effort to connect with him, and to understand him—that was empathetic. Empathy is not something that magically happens, but something you do. It's a living thing, and it comes alive through communication. While we were connected on the call, it ran back and forth across the space between us, occasionally stumbling, sometimes soaring—a process of trying, failing, and trying again. Whether he felt understood, and whether he experienced that as empathy, I'll never know for sure.

He spoke an ocean of grief into existence. I tried to swim into it, the waves lapping at my knees, bracing myself against the cold to show him that I was not afraid. I felt my way into his experience, imperfectly, and only as far as he could let me in a half hour call. The ocean was much bigger than I could ever comprehend; but I hoped that, at least for a moment, he could somehow feel that he wasn't alone at its wide, blue edge.

2

Empathy is humble

"Cheer up, love!" As a woman with a naturally stoic resting face, I can't begin to count the number of times I've heard this phrase throughout my life—nor to explain how much it frustrates me each time. Ever since childhood, I've felt a bristling annoyance when other people make inferences about how I'm feeling based on the way I look or speak. This may be unfair of me—some of these people are only attempting to be friendly—but it's rooted in a deep emotional wound. The cumulative effect of always having your feelings misread, like being told to "cheer up" when you're feeling fine, is to never feel truly seen.

The outer signals of autistic bodies don't always align

with what we're feeling internally (at least, not in ways that a non-autistic eye might be able to see). Flapping hands might be an expression of joy, rather than anxiety or overwhelm. Silence might be a peaceful retreat, rather than a sulk or an attempt to be passive-aggressive. Expressionless faces and slow responses might be the result of a brain that's running on fumes, trying desperately to process layers of information—even if, to the outside observer, it looks like total vacancy. Simply getting through the day as an autistic person, trying to swerve the attempts to misinterpret your mood or misattribute your actions, can be exhausting.

This experience of being mis-seen is not just unique to my experience as an autistic person, but something that all marginalized people face. People of color, disabled people, queer people, and anyone else who exists in the minority will know the experience of being viewed through the critical eye of the majority. For autistic people with multiple intersecting marginalized identities, the daily navigation of other people's assumptions might look something like Keanu Reeves dodging bullets in *The Matrix*. The autistic self-advocate Catina Burkett has written about how racist and ableist stereotypes dovetail together to create a perception of her as an "angry black woman." "Such cultural stereotypes make it particularly dangerous to be 'autistic while black,'" she writes. "In the workplace, I am often criticized for the way I carry myself. I am told that my calm, relaxed energy comes off as superior and naive, and

Empathy is humble

that my assertiveness looks like aggression."[1]

Assuming that you know how someone is feeling is not empathy. Even when the intention is ostensibly good—for example, swooping in with what you believe to be soothing advice or reassurance—your kindness may not land well if you haven't checked how that person is feeling first. I'd always rather be asked about how I'm doing before attempts to rescue me. Otherwise, I'm left cringing at the dissonant clash between how I genuinely feel, and how I'm being perceived.

As a therapist, one of the core tenets of the empathy I try to practice is that I cannot assume anything about others. There is some nuance to this. Of course, part of what I do is track the things that a client is telling me unconsciously, as well as consciously. For example, I might pick up on the uncomfortable shift in the chair as someone tells me how happy they are, or the minor key of sadness that chimes through their voice as they claim to be "fine." But when I pick up on these signals, I take them as brushstrokes, not the whole picture. I ask my client how they're feeling, checking whether what I'm sensing aligns with their experience.

This process should be tentative and curious, and always come from a place of humility. Yet this is at odds with one of science's most dominant explanations of empathy, which sees empathy as underpinned by the psychological ability, "Theory of Mind." This magical trait—sometimes referred to as "mind-reading"—is supposedly the root of our capacity to empathize with others. It has also been cited as the component of empathy that autistic and other neurodivergent people may be "lacking." But to see empathy as reducible to a psychological trick is to belie the gentle exploration between two people that empathy really is.

In this chapter, we'll explore the roots of the outdated Theory of Mind, and how it has been used to try to explain autistic and other neurodivergent people's supposed deficit in empathy. We'll also touch on the emerging theories—primarily the "double empathy problem"—that are shaping a new understanding of empathy through the lens of communication, rather than psychology.

Where is my (theory of) mind?

The term "Theory of Mind" is used to describe the ability to understand that other people have minds of their own, and to imagine what they might be thinking. Psychologists have long related this capacity—which I'll abbreviate to ToM—to so-called cognitive empathy, or the ability to take the perspective of others. It's been referred to as "mind-reading," a term used by autism researchers,[2] and as "mentalizing," a term that emerged from psychoanalytic work with patients with borderline personality disorder.[3] It's sometimes described as the ability to "think about thinking."

If I were to take a stab at thinking about what you're thinking right now, I'd say it's something along the lines of, so far, this all sounds relatively inoffensive. What's so bad about studying how we think about our own mental states, and the mental states of others? It's true that mentalizing can be a helpful idea, particularly in psychotherapy, where therapists can support clients in developing their ability to step back and think about their own thought processes and those of others. But, despite ToM being described as "one of the quintessential abilities that makes us human,"[4] it has long been suggested that some humans don't possess it. The ideas of "mind-reading" and "mentalizing" grew out of research on neurodivergent people—primarily autistic people and those with personality disorders—because researchers were looking for the deficit in those people. It has been suggested that ToM is the "missing device" in autistic brains leading to a lack of empathy, despite there being little empirical evidence to support this idea. The suggestion that some people possess a magical mind-reading quality was predicated, from the start, on the idea that some people don't.

According to psychology textbooks, due to our inability to mind-read, autistic people are only able to view other people as objects. In *The Encyclopedia of Neuropsychological Disorders*, it's suggested that for an autistic person, trying to determine how someone felt by looking at their face would be "like looking at the headlights of a car to determine why the car just did what it did."[5] Leading autism researcher Uta Frith once wrote: "Imagine the way we interact with a cash machine, and then imagine how we interact with another person. An autistic person would not see much difference between the two situations."[6] In my favorite example—so repulsive that it leaves me caught somewhere between laughter and tears—developmental psychologist Alison Gopnik once imagined that autistic people view other human beings as "noisy skin-bags."[7]

These descriptions of autistic people's inner worlds, as described by non-autistic researchers, were not written generations ago, in an unimaginably distant history. They were written between 1995 and 2012. These statements take the idea of mind-reading to its most extreme conclusion: Those who lack ToM are compared to animals or robots, freaks who view our fellow human beings as a confusing mess of machinery and skin. It is laughable that this theory rests on the idea that we view other people as objects, when the theory is itself so objectifying. Who is really being viewed as a "noisy skin-bag": the researcher through the eyes of the autistic person, or the autistic person through the eyes of the researcher?

The ToM model of autism has been roundly debunked, and autistic activists, self-advocates, and academics have been calling out the bad science behind it for decades. And yet, while training to become a psychotherapist in the 2020s, I was dismayed to encounter the hulking poltergeist of ToM in texts I read and lectures I attended. The idea that some people are "missing" this ability to read minds still clings to popular culture and to academia, despite many attempts to consign it to history books.

Beyond what this means for autistic people, the idea of ToM as a necessary component of empathy has implications for us all. ToM is a strangely cold, mechanical conceptualization of what it means to relate to other people. It makes machines of all of us: It turns the ability to care and connect and commiserate, our fluid, surprising relationships with each other, into a "module" of the brain that can be either switched on or off. This is a deeply individualistic, and strangely technological, way of thinking about thinking.

In reality, our nonverbal communication or sense of empathetic attunement is often built on the sharing of social or cultural norms. What psychology describes as a missing mechanism of our brains is really a manifestation of cultural difference—people with different systems of communication from one another are less equipped to read each other's signals. It makes no sense to attribute these misunderstandings to a psychological "deficit," rather than a case of crossed wires. Ironically, those of us who are accused of lacking the capacity to read minds, and who are so used to finding ourselves on the wrong side of these misunderstandings, might be more aware of this need for humility and open-mindedness when communicating than those who find themselves in the majority.

If we free ourselves from the idea of ToM, we gain the space to radically reimagine what empathy can be. Removing our certainty that we are equipped to understand the minds of others gives us the freedom to discover and surprise each other. Rather than stick to the dehumanizing scripts of psychological theories, we can humbly open ourselves up to the uncharted territory of the other.

The theory that won't die

"Why is it so slow to die?" That's the question that Dr. Chloe Farahar can't contain, when I tell them how surprised I was to encounter Theory of Mind in my psychotherapy training. Chloe laughs sardonically. As they put it, "psychology, and a lot of the sciences, are not that good at filtering down latest understandings. Once something's out there, it's really hard to retract." In other words, there's a sunk-cost fallacy at play. To abandon the idea of ToM now, when it is so entrenched that it shapes the direction of a lot of research, would be costly, embarrassing, and even existentially threatening to the industry of psychology.

Chloe is a social psychologist who is currently researching the mental health experiences of young neurodivergent people. They also deliver training on autism for NHS professionals, and have run support groups for autistic adults. When Chloe was completing their degree in psychology in the early 2010s, they remember having only one class about autism. In this class, they were taught about the Theory of Mind model, along with other impairment- and deficit-based models of autism. At the time, Chloe didn't know that they were autistic; it was something they began to question only after graduating.

Now, from their position as an out and proud autistic person and a post-doctoral researcher, Chloe makes no bones about asserting their view on ToM. "Even if we ignored how dehumanizing and dangerous a theory it is," they say, "if we purely looked at the science of it, it is a terrible theory."

To understand how we got to this point, and the role ToM has played in shaping our dominant cultural concept of empathy, it's worth looking back at the history of ToM as an idea. Psychologists David Premack and Guy Woodruff were the first ones to describe ToM, while researching the psychology of primates in the 1970s. In a paper titled "Does the chimpanzee have a theory of mind?," Premack and Woodruff sought to find out if chimpanzees could recognize when a person needs something. The paper asserted: "In assuming that other individuals *want*, *think*, *believe*, and the like, one infers states that are not directly observable.... These inferences, which amount to a theory of mind, are, to our knowledge, universal in human adults."[8]

A few years later, developmental psychologists set about proving that this assumed skill was not, in fact, universal in humans. In 1985, Simon Baron-Cohen, Alan Leslie, and Uta Frith published their seminal paper, "Does the autistic child have a 'theory of mind'?" It is notable that the title of the paper directly mirrors Premack and Woodruff's, replacing "chimpanzee" with "autistic child." While it may be nothing but an unfortunate coincidence, I can't help but read this as revealing of how autistic children are dehumanized under the fluorescent glare of science.

Baron-Cohen, Leslie, and Frith's paper is massively influential. It is still referenced, to this day, in pretty much anything you read that claims that autistic people have a cognitive empathy deficit. The paper begins by explaining that the core feature of autism is "failure to develop normal social relationships." The researchers set out their hypothesis that this may be caused by an impairment in ToM. To test this hypothesis, they carried out a study with twenty autistic children, fourteen children with Down syndrome, and twenty-seven children who were described as "clinically normal." The autistic children included in the study were a "high functioning subgroup," which means that they all had a relatively high IQ and no learning disability. The paper describes what happened when these children were all given what is now commonly referred to as "the Sally-Anne test."

The Sally-Anne test is perhaps the most famous psychological test devised to determine whether someone has ToM—or can read minds. To carry out the test, a scene is acted out, either by two researchers or using dolls. One character in the scene is named Sally, and the other is named Anne. Sally puts a marble into a basket. Sally then leaves the room. While Sally is gone, Anne takes the marble out of the basket and puts it in a box. Finally, Sally returns.

At this critical point, the researcher then asks their test subject: "Where will Sally look for her marble?"

The idea behind this test is that, if you have ToM, you are aware that other people have separate minds to your own, and so they might not know the same things that you know. With this ability, you would know that, when Sally comes back into the room, she still thinks that the marble is in the basket. You saw Anne move the marble, but you know that Sally didn't see this. Hence, this test is known as a kind of "false-belief" test—because it's testing your ability to understand that other people can hold false beliefs.

In Baron-Cohen, Leslie, and Frith's flagship 1985 study with twenty autistic children, sixteen of those children failed this test. When they were asked, "Where will Sally look for her marble?"—while the "normal" children and the children with Down syndrome consistently pointed to the location that Sally had last seen the marble—the majority of the autistic children pointed to the box, the actual location of the marble. "We therefore conclude that the autistic children did not appreciate the difference between their own and the doll's knowledge," the researchers stated. "Our results strongly support the hypothesis that autistic children as a group fail to employ a theory of mind.... and are thus at a grave disadvantage when having to predict the behavior of other people."[9]

Despite the definitive tone of this conclusion and the ubiquitous application of this paper's findings, this is far from an open and shut case. Of the twenty autistic children tested in Baron-Cohen and co.'s original research, four were found to pass the test. This is a pass rate of 20 percent. The researchers argue that this is because ToM may not be impaired in 100 percent of autistic people, or may be impaired to different degrees, but that autistic people in general may be significantly more likely to have a ToM deficit. If this were the case, then we would expect to see this reflected in test results over and over again. But there have been multiple attempts to repeat the original Sally-Anne test that have largely failed to produce the same results found in 1985.[10]

This failure to find a consistent and convincing deficit in autistic people could be down to the small sample sizes that this theory is based on. It never fails to astound me when I remember that this entire theory sprang from the results of studying only twenty autistic children—four of whom were found to pass. This sample size isn't big enough to definitively determine anything about such a large population of people, particularly a group as heterogenous and complex as autistic people. Those twenty children are unlikely to be representative of autistic people as a whole, particularly when you consider the "WEIRD" bias of psychological studies (Western, Educated, Industrialized, Rich, and Democratic). White, middle class, "high-functioning" autistic boys are massively overrepresented in autism research. We cannot draw universal conclusions from studies that look only at this part of the population.

Over the decades, researchers have continued to test

the ToM hypothesis by devising other, more elaborate tests with the aim of discovering whether test subjects can not only understand that other people may have false beliefs, but also that other people might have false beliefs about others' false beliefs. These are called second-order false-belief tests. (For example, rather than be asked where you thought Sally might look for the marble, you could be asked where a third character thought Sally would look.) In one 1989 study, autistic children who were found to "pass" first-order false-belief tests like the Sally-Anne test were recruited for a second-order false-belief test, which they failed. The researchers concluded that, even if autistic children "have developed a theory of mind at the lower level [they] are nevertheless specifically delayed in the acquisition of a more complex theory of mind."[11]

However, further studies showed that some autistic children could also pass second-order false-belief tests. In the 1990s, researcher Francesca Happé responded to this discrepancy by devising what she called "an advanced test of theory of mind," referred to in shorthand as the Strange Stories test. Happé's test involved telling twenty-four stories to autistic children, and then asking them questions about the characters' thoughts and feelings. In the stories, characters do something unexpected—such as tell a white lie by saying an aunt looks good in her ugly hat—and respondents are asked to explain the characters' motivations. The autistic subjects were found to be "impaired at providing context-appropriate mental state explanations for the story characters' nonliteral utterances."[12] At the turn of the millennium, Happé collaborated with other researchers to devise another test of ToM. This time, autistic children were asked to watch animations of triangles moving around a screen, and then describe what the triangles were doing. The autistic children were found to attribute "inappropriate" descriptions to the triangles' behavior—for example, in one sequence, the researchers were looking for the children to describe a triangle as "coaxing" another, but an autistic child described it as "being cheeky."[13] And so, we had another novel way in which autistic children could be said to lack empathy: by not being able to read the minds of two-dimensional shapes. Other tests have looked for ToM deficits by assessing how well someone can identify another person's emotions by looking at a photo of their eyes (the Reading the Mind in the Eyes test),[14] or whether they can select the correct ending to a comic strip depicting a social interaction (the Comic Strip test).[15]

Autistic academic M. Remi Yergeau and psychologist Morton Ann Gernsbacher, in a thorough takedown of the ToM model of autism, describe the development of these ever more complex false-belief tests as a "methodological arms race." In their view, over the last few decades, researchers have developed increasingly complicated ToM measures when the previous trials have failed to definitively prove that autistic people lack a ToM.[16] This is effectively moving the goalposts. If you can pass a false-belief test, can you interpret these animated triangles? If you can correctly identify emotions from photographs of eyes, can you accurately describe a story? Additionally, over the years, when autistic people have been found to pass ToM tasks, researchers have often explained this away by suggesting that we must be finding alternative workarounds in order to compensate for our lack of ToM.[17]

The findings of these escalating tests have fluctuated—some studies have found that 10 percent of autistic participants can pass false-belief tests, while others have found that as many as 50 percent of their autistic sample can pass.[18] Like the original Sally-Anne test, many of the second-order false-belief tests have failed to produce the same results in further studies. Happé's Strange Stories test findings have similarly failed to replicate.[19] Blurring the overall picture even further is the fact that there are other groups of people who are also frequently found to fail the tests. Deaf children, blind children, and children with learning disabilities, cerebral palsy, and Down syndrome have all been found to fail false-belief tests.[20] Rather than conclude that all of these populations struggle with empathy and intuiting the thoughts and feelings of other people, it seems much more likely that communication differences are at play.

In fact, some scientists have demonstrated that when children fail false-belief tests, it may be because they simply don't understand the questions being asked of them. One study has shown that when a group of autistic children are compared with non-autistic children with the same language ability, their seeming differences in ToM evaporate.[21] As the autistic self-advocate Rachel Cohen-Rottenberg—a passionate critic of ToM model of autism who authored the blog *Autism and Empathy* in the 2000s and early 2010s—has pointed out, many autistic people struggle with verbal communication because of our differences in sensory and auditory processing. In a critique of the ToM model, she imagined that she herself would struggle with the test, and would perform better if she could see the questions written down.[22] It's not surprising that being interrogated with syntactically complicated questions by an intimidating researcher would be a confusing situation for many autistic children. Notably, when the test has been repeated in a non-linguistic format, using drawings instead of words, both autistic and Deaf children have been found to outperform their hearing peers.[23]

Most importantly of all, if we set aside the unconvincing data behind the argument that autistic people "lack" ToM, there are some valid critiques of the concept of ToM more broadly. Psychologists Ivan Leudar and Alan Costall have been vocally skeptical of ToM since the 1990s. They point out that equating "having" ToM with the ability to pass a false-belief test is a massive oversimplification of how human development works.[24] ToM is a much bigger and broader concept than is measured by the Sally-Anne test. Take this description of ToM from Baron-Cohen's book *Autism and Asperger Syndrome: The Facts*:

When we see someone else turn to look out of the window, we typically infer that they must have *seen* something of *interest*, and that they might *know* about something that we cannot presently see. It might even be something that they *want*. Notice that in this interpretation, we have gone beyond mere behavior to imagine a whole set of *mental states* that link up in the other person's mind. When we . . . use a ToM, we can not only make sense of another person's behavior (why did their head swivel on their neck? Why did their eyes move left?), but we can predict what they might do next."[25]

This is a complex process with many steps. ToM is said to be behind our ability to infer the thoughts, intentions, desires, and feelings of another person, and to use this information to make sense of and predict their behavior. To say that autistic people can't do any of this because they can't predict that Sally knows where to look for a marble seems far-fetched. This is partly why so many other tests for ToM have been developed, including the Strange Stories test and the Reading the Mind in the Eyes test—ToM is a much vaster concept than can be accurately captured by one simple test. The result is that we have many tests, each of them measuring a slightly different ability, and yet, all claim to prove one central, unified concept.

The false-belief tests, and other tests presented to

autistic children, were done so in order to prove the hypothesis that these children could not imagine the minds of others. The absurdity of this occurred to me one day while I was speaking to my partner, Ruby, about their dog. Ruby's dog is a very smart young boy, who lets us know when he wants to go outside to use the bathroom by ringing a bell that hangs by the front door. One day, in the early months of our relationship, I was dog-sitting and noticed that he hadn't rung the bell all morning. In fact, he had never rung the bell while I was taking care of him alone.

"Perhaps he thinks I don't know what the bell means," I mused to Ruby, semi-seriously, when they came home. They laughed, and agreed that this might be the case.

"He probably thinks that he is the one taking care of you today," Ruby suggested. "And he's been taking his job very seriously. No bathroom breaks."

"Or maybe he thinks I'm a little slow and don't know how to operate the front door," I riffed. "As he's never seen me do it."

After this conversation, it dawned on me that Ruby and I were assigning "Theory of Mind" to the dog in this scenario. In doing so, we were humanizing him—a literal dog—to a greater extent than some autism researchers have humanized the children they study.

This brought home to me the gross unfairness of this quest to scientifically codify empathy. The autistic children who have been studied for their lack of ToM were doomed to fail from the start. The scientists set out to look for the faulty cog in our machinery. The whole enterprise, from designing the tests to interpreting the data, was a search for a problem (a problem that is assumed the researchers themselves don't have—even as they fail to empathize with their test subjects). The ToM model of autism looks at the autistic person through a normative eye. It makes an assumption about us, and in the process, blocks the outsider's ability to empathize with us.

This is a problem that hounds all of psychology: the paradox of psychologists positioning themselves outside of humanity and "objectively" assessing what it means to be human. ToM evangelists assert that people, in general, make clumsy guesses and inferences about others' inner worlds, while implying that psychologists know perfectly well what is happening in the minds of others.[26] After all, the word "theory" in "Theory of Mind" is referring to the idea that we can only ever theorize about what is happening in the thoughts of others. We can't know for sure. Of course, this raises the question: If none of us can know for sure, then how do *psychologists* know for sure?

Summarizing this idea, with tongue firmly in cheek, the autistic academic M. Remi Yergeau defines "Theory of Mind" as: "The theory that some minds can't know the minds of those who invented Theory of Mind: even though the minds who invented Theory of Mind can't know the minds of those who lack Theory of Mind, they do not lack Theory of Mind because, dude, they invented Theory of Mind."[27]

It's important to highlight the damage done by the ToM model of autism, because the idea of mind-reading in itself has become a barrier to empathy. When we assume that some people struggle with cognitive empathy, or thinking about thinking, we see those people as somehow "broken" or disordered, and lacking in a quality that makes them "quintessentially human." These assumptions are damaging to those people, but also to all of us, as they hinder our ability to get closer to one another.

All of which returns us to psychologist Chloe Farahar's question: Why will the theory not die? It lumbers on, still rearing its head in university teaching and academic journals in the 2020s, where its unchecked assumptions impact all of us. We'd do better to leave it consigned to the past, and to focus instead on newer, more inclusive conceptualizations of empathy.

The double empathy problem

The key to better connection lies not with the outdated ToM model, but with its biggest challenger in recent years: the "double empathy problem." This idea was first proposed in 2012 by Dr. Damian Milton. His theory rips up the individualistic premise of the ToM by arguing that empathy is not a feature of psychology, but of relationships.

As a sociologist, Milton's work throughout the 2000s was grounded in Marxist and phenomenological theory—"phenomenology" being the philosophical perspective that there is no objective "reality," but that each of us forms our own reality. This philosophy underpinned Milton's early writings, arguing that society and our unique social positions construct our individual worldviews and how we relate to one another.[28] Then, in 2009, Milton's own world changed when he found out that his son was autistic—and later that he was, too.

Becoming immersed in the world of neurodiversity advocacy, Milton joined the dots between his own philosophy and the work of autistic activists and self-advocates like Jim Sinclair, who had long been arguing that neurotypical people fail to empathize with autistic people just as much as autistic people fail to empathize with them. This is when Milton began giving talks at conferences about "the double empathy problem." His big idea was that breakdowns in empathy arise not from "disordered" individuals, but from two-way failures of communication between people coming from fundamentally different points of view.

By this logic, autistic people have an "empathy deficit" only when they are interacting with non-autistic people, and the reverse is also true: Non-autistic people struggle to take the perspectives of autistic people. When you match people with their own neurotypes, these so-called empathy problems tend to dissipate. Milton's conclusion is that there are communication differences between non-autistic people and autistic people that make empathy harder, rather than there being any innate dysfunction in the brains of autistic people.[29]

Milton was among the first to point out a glaring fact: that while there had been decades of research into why autistic people misunderstand neurotypicals, we hadn't been talking about the fact that neurotypical people also tend to misunderstand autistic people. Milton wrote in 2012 that while psychology lauds the average neurotypical person's apparent ability to "assume understandings" of other people, it's apparent that "when such 'empathy' is applied toward an 'autistic person' . . . it is often wildly inaccurate in its measure."[30]

The double empathy problem gets to the heart of the issue with the ToM model of empathy: There are always a minimum of two people involved in an interaction. So if an interaction goes wrong and a miscommunication takes place, why do we assume only one of them is to blame? This is not only true for autistic people, but for anyone who's found themselves feeling unheard or misunderstood when they've become tangled in cultural or communication differences. You cannot build an authentic relationship on the assumption that everyone is singing from the same hymn sheet when it comes to social norms and values. What's seen as a lack of empathy can often be put down to an encounter of different cultural, social, or linguistic norms—an idea we will explore in more depth in chapter 5.

Other academics have sought to explain or identify

exactly what these communication differences are between neurodivergent and neurotypical people. Linguistics researcher Rachel Cullen argues that a key difference in autistic communication is rooted in language: Autistic people communicate literally and explicitly, while non-autistic people rely heavily on contextual clues and implication.[31]

When they're training professionals in neurodiversity awareness, Chloe Farahar explains this theory with a simple exercise. Pretending to be thinking of an activity, Chloe will ask the room, "Does anyone have a pen?" When, as inevitably happens, multiple people in the room try to offer up a pen, Chloe asks, "Why are you trying to hand me a pen?" Often, the reply comes, "Because you asked for one." But Chloe didn't ask for a pen—they asked, *"Does anyone have* a pen?," to which the answer would be "yes" or "no."

"When you're communicating with an autistic person, you have to be specific," Chloe explains. "Those extra-specific words will mean the communication is less likely to break down, and we're less likely to be seen as obtuse and rude because we didn't hand you a pen when you asked for one—because *you didn't ask*!"

This idea is fresh and exciting because it provides a simple, practically applicable framework for how to approach communication in a way that is more inclusive. Rather than demonize autistic people for being pathologically unable to pick up on subtext, it presents our more literal communication style as a neutral difference, and suggests a way in which this difference can be accommodated. Unlike the ToM model of autism, Cullen's hypothesis is hopeful: It offers one simple way for autistic and non-autistic people to decode one another. And it shares the load more evenly. As Chloe says, "Non-autistic people have some responsibility to be curious and nonjudgmental about our differences, to help bridge the gap between us, because we're already disabled and working really hard in an environment that's overwhelming us. So, non-autistic people need to take some responsibility, if not *more* responsibility."

Of course, this argument isn't only academic to Chloe. It hits home personally. Like many other autistic people, before they identified as autistic, Chloe was used to being told that they came across to others as cold or rude. They internalized these negative ideas about themself, and were left feeling as though they were somehow broken or wrong for the way they behaved socially. One of the most poignant examples of this, they share with me, happened in the aftermath of their father's death. Chloe lost their father suddenly, at the age of twenty-two. Chloe explains that when they're navigating a crisis, they cope by going into what they describe as "logical mode"—they prioritize the tasks that need to be done, and will delay their emotional processing until later. For Chloe, this looked like making lists, calling funeral homes, and generally taking on the practical tasks of managing the aftermath of a death. On the outside, Chloe appeared cool and collected, even if on the inside, they were falling apart. Other relatives read this as a lack of emotion. "My aunt, talking to my sister, was saying how cold and uncaring and unfeeling I was. That lack of empathy and perspective-taking from my aunt really impacted me. It hurt to feel and think that other people could view me in that way. Because that was a really distressing, traumatic experience."

Chloe notes that in that situation, rather than make a judgment about how they were feeling from outside observations, their aunt could have just asked them. That small gesture would have helped the two to communicate with one another, and made Chloe feel understood and supported. "This is the big issue, I would say, in non-autistic and autistic communication breakdown," says Chloe. "Because that's what we're talking about really—communication breakdown."

As the double empathy problem makes clear, communication is a two-way street, and so empathetic failures can't be one person's alone. In a thorough critique of the ToM model of autism back in 2005, academic David Smukler noted: "Both communication and social interaction, by definition, require more than one person, and difficulties in either area should properly be located between individuals and not within one individual."[32] When Chloe's aunt made an assumption about how Chloe was feeling based on external appearances, this was not a failure of Chloe's.

Putting in the work to learn about another person means avoiding shortcuts that make assumptions about them. But, in day-to-day life, people take such shortcuts all the time. They find it easier to relate to people who behave in the same ways they do, and can be quick to pathologize or "other" people who act differently. When someone communicates in a way that falls outside of what's considered "normal," this is a real opportunity to stretch your empathy muscles, to stay humble and curious. Your empathy is not tested by the people who are just like you, and who communicate in the way you expect. The real test of your empathy is how you respond to those who surprise you, those who test you, and those who you don't immediately feel you understand.

Navigating each other

Empathy is seeking to know the other, not believing that we already know them. So much of autism research has, for decades, made assumptions about the autistic experience, rather than exploring our point of view. This is a power dynamic that replicates itself in a million tiny judgments made toward people in the minority every day, as they move among the majority. Communication involves guesswork and leaps of faith, but it also, necessarily, means having the humility to know that our guesses may not be accurate, and to allow people to tell us or show us how they really feel.

Empathy is humble

Someone who taught me about empathizing without assumptions was Rosie—one of three nonspeaking autistic children I supported on a day out to Blackpool beach, while volunteering for a disability charity. The children were aged between six and eight, and had all been transfixed by the mottled colorful lights of the aquarium, and squealed at the squelch of sand between their toes. As the day on the wind-whipped seafront drew on, the children grew more tired, and some warning signs of sensory overload began to show. I, together with four other volunteers, tried my best to remain nonchalant under the tutting gazes of passersby, who shook their heads disapprovingly as Rosie unleashed ear-piercing screams.

Sensing that everyone had hit their limit and that it was, fairly urgently, time to head home, we bundled the children back into the cars we'd arrived in. While our driver disappeared to pay the parking fee, another volunteer and I waited with Rosie in the car. It was a hot day, and the air felt like a duvet that had been packed into the back of the car with us. In the thick heat, Rosie began to have a full meltdown. The overpowering force of an autistic meltdown is fearsome: Having had many myself, I knew something of the internal explosion that Rosie was experiencing.

Meltdowns are intense, bodily responses to being overwhelmed. From the outside, they are sometimes described as similar to tantrums. A meltdown might look like screaming, crying, thrashing, rocking, or self-injuring. When I'm having a meltdown, the feeling of having skin becomes infuriating. Everything is a nerve ending, and nothing helps. The weight of the overload on me is existential and all-consuming. It's different for everyone, but during my own meltdowns, I feel the irrepressible urge to seek out some kind of huge sensory input—to be crushed, flattened, defused like a bomb, something that physically matches the intensity of what I'm going through emotionally. I felt a kind of kinship as I watched Rosie rock and scream in her car seat, wailing at the pitch of an emergency siren, the color red flaring across her face. The charity I was volunteering with had trained me to offer calm, distanced support, and never to restrain the young people I worked with. So I sat back without touching Rosie, offering her what I hoped were some soothing words. But when Rosie, as autistic children often do, thrashed her limbs wildly, she accidentally connected her fist with my cheekbone. In response to this furious, bone-against-bone pain, I let out a sharp yelp.

Rosie ever-so-briefly paused in her thrashing, her fresh tears cutting trails through the surface of the dried ones on her cheeks. She sobbed as she leaned toward me, and in the exact throbbing spot where she had just hit me, lightly kissed me on the cheek. Though she couldn't speak, I could hear notes of regret and guilt in her muffled wails. I felt that I recognized, in Rosie, the waves of humiliation and anger I had experienced in my own past meltdowns: how I hated my own behavior, even as I felt I couldn't control it or stop myself from doing it.

Empathy is humble

But most of all, in that moment, I felt Rosie's love and care. It softened the instinctive annoyance and frustration that I felt when her hand painfully collided with my face. Her gesture told me that to her, I was not simply an object in the way of her meltdown. She knew that I was me, that I experienced pain, and that she had caused me pain. She seemed sorry for hurting me and hadn't wanted it to happen. Even in the midst of the excruciating, mind-flattening hell of a meltdown, she was able to express that to me through a kiss.

I'm not inside Rosie's mind, and I can't know what she was actually thinking and feeling in this moment. I feel that I can partly relate to her experience, having also experienced sensory overload and meltdowns, but I'm also a very different person with different needs. So, while I held my own past experiences in mind, I also tried not to project this on to her by assuming what she was feeling. Instead, I tried to make myself open to what Rosie was communicating through her behavior: her frustration, her overwhelm, her apology. I was applying something called the total communication approach, which is a style of supporting people with complex needs that recognizes everything as a potential, non-traditional way of communicating. In this approach, gestures, movements, sounds, and even violent meltdowns or so-called "challenging behavior" can all be a way of telling you something. You just need to meet that behavior with curiosity about what you're being told.

Of course, if someone is screaming at a painful volume or even being violent, you may not always be in the most charitably curious mood. It's called challenging behavior for a reason—it challenges. But the default assumption about children who behave in these ways is that they are naughty or bad; their intentions are read as malicious. I felt that the tutting older people we encountered on Blackpool's seafront that day saw Rosie like this, as they openly expressed their disdain when the storm clouds of her meltdown began to darken. More than the shock of her punch, I felt dehumanized by the long glances those people cast our way, their judgment hanging in the air like a bad smell. To them, it seemed Rosie was little more than a naughty child, or a nuisance.

This experience is reflected in many of the guides for parents and caregivers on how to handle the meltdowns of autistic children—the advice given is to try not to be affected or embarrassed by the disdain of onlookers.[33] The behavior of the young people is made only more challenging and distressing by the harsh reactions of people surrounding them. In the eye of the storm with Rosie, I knew that there was so much more to her than judgmental passersby could see. Medical theorizing about autistic minds says that we cannot fully conceptualize other people—that we are inherently selfish, seeing others as little more than "noisy skin-bags." But every single one of us, autistic or not, has the capacity to dehumanize others in this way when we allow our experience of each other to be colored

Empathy is humble

by stereotypes and assumptions.

Rather than trying to locate one another using theories like dusty old maps, we might allow ourselves to approach connection as though it's a more ancient style of navigation: feeling the direction of the wind on our skin, or observing the shadow of moss on a tree. We might read implicit signals from one another, check our understanding of those signals tentatively, and be willing to be corrected or surprised. Often, we will get it wrong. This can be humbling, vulnerable work. But allowing ourselves to wander off the beaten path together can take us to greener, brighter places than the maps told us existed.

3

Empathy is embodied

The scream of a person in pain hits my spine like a lightning bolt hitting a tree. On the top deck of a London bus one cold morning, I'm ripped away from my mindless gazing out the windows as I hear the violent yell, and every one of my nerve endings comes alive in response to the sound. And yet, despite this visceral response, I find myself unable to move from my seat.

A woman had fallen, with a sickening thud, from the top deck to the bottom when the bus driver quite suddenly hit the brakes. The bus lurched, the woman's body hurtled out of sight, and a handful of passengers—including my partner at the time—leapt to their feet and ran to see that she was okay with a total lack of hesitation.

It soon became apparent that the woman was shocked, but not seriously hurt. The sound had been worse than the fall. Still, out of an abundance of caution, the driver stopped the bus and an ambulance was called. My boyfriend and I waited, along with the startled woman, the driver, and another passenger, to see her safely into the hands of the paramedics. Then we continued with the rest of our day, heading into central London to meet our friends.

Later, unable to sleep, I punished myself by replaying the incident again and again in my mind, like the worn-out VHS tapes of my childhood. I felt embarrassed by my passivity in the face of a crisis. If I was an empathetic person, as I hoped I was, then why did I freeze when someone needed my help? Why was it that I could feel the impact of another person screaming in pain, flashing like a red light through my nervous system, and yet I couldn't translate that feeling into action?

Scrambling to make sense of this puzzle, my mind had a lot of answers, but none of them seemed sufficient. The first explanation I reached for: I don't like to be crowded or touched when I've hurt myself, because it makes an already overwhelming situation feel even more intense. So when I see someone else hurt themselves, I somewhat instinctively hold back from crowding them—even though they likely feel differently about it than I do.

I also tend to be quite pragmatic. When I know there's nothing I can offer of practical use in a situation, I don't

Empathy is embodied

offer my help. I've learned, over the years, that this can be considered rude or callous. You're supposed to be seen to *want* to offer your help, even if you know that there's not really anything you can do that isn't already being done. In this instance, I saw that my partner and others were already running toward the fallen woman, and I didn't know—practically—what else I would be able to do that would be of any use.

Along with this caution and pragmatism, I have a mind that processes things a beat or two slower than other people's. In social situations, I can feel that I'm tripping over my own feet to keep up with what's happening. Sometimes, I feel like I haven't really taken in what's happened in an interaction until it's over—especially if I'm surprised or overwhelmed. When something happens suddenly, it can take me longer than it would take other people to react, as though I'm running on a delay.

These were all ways in which my autistic traits might in some way account for my apparent lack of empathy toward the injured woman on the bus that day. But none of these explanations felt adequate, and so I kept on looking for answers. I was doing what I often did as a way of coping: intellectualizing and ruminating on my feelings, instead of wholly feeling them. Beneath the endless chatter of theories was a deep, incessant drumbeat of shame.

Looking back, what this story reveals to me is that empathy involves our whole bodyminds. I couldn't find an intellectual answer for my failure to act when I was startled on the bus, because the answer was not just in my mind—it was in my body. We've all heard of "fight or flight," the tendency to either run away or fight back when a traumatic response is triggered. Newer additions to the list include "fawn" (another word for appeasing, or people-pleasing) and "freeze." My response on the bus, as is common for me in distressing situations, was to freeze. Beginning to understand this and to develop a compassionate self-awareness of my bodily feelings was the key to start unlocking a conscious practice of empathy.

In this chapter, we'll look at why our new understanding of empathy needs to be liberated from the idea of "mind–body dualism" that says our thoughts and emotions are separate, and instead recognize that empathy is embodied. We'll start by taking a look at the inconclusive search for empathy in the brain, and the debunked idea that empathy is a trait of the "female brain." A more inclusive idea of empathy moves beyond these restrictive, biologically determinist binaries. Recognizing the role that the body plays in empathy also means recognizing how trauma shapes our capacity to empathize and build relationships.

There is no specific empathy "gadget" in my mind that accounts for moments when I fail to connect with others. It is a hallmark of Western culture to prize thinking over feeling, and to separate the two processes. Rather than separate the brain from the rest of the body, we can see our bodyminds as holistic systems, constantly experiencing, sensing, evolving, and connecting. Empathy does not sit discretely in our minds, like a graphics card or a line of code. It's a living process that involves the entirety of our beings.

Searching for the empathy gadget

If there was an empathy gadget in the brain, where would it be? Scientists have been seeking the answer to this question for decades. Neuroscience really took off in the 1990s, dubbed the "Decade of the Brain" by President George H. W. Bush, who declared that there would be a focus on raising public awareness of brain science from 1990 to 1999.

This decade brought the advent of fMRI imaging: those color-coded, gently glowing brain scans you may have seen replicated in newspapers and popular science articles over the past thirty years. These scans gave scientists a brand-new way to look directly into the human brain. Previously, they had been able to carry out tests only on dead, damaged human brains or living animal ones, or to make conclusions based on psychological tests. It was impossible to carry out invasive physical tests on a living human brain, because of the obvious ethical problems. But, with fMRI brain scans, we had the next best thing: a scan that could visually show where blood is flowing in the brain. By tracking blood flow, scientists could show which areas of the brain are the most "active" at any given time. This opened the floodgates for studies using fMRI scans that attempted to "map" various emotions and processes in the brain, to see which parts were most active when people felt, for example, angry or afraid.

The hype that surrounded this new technology brought with it a lot of bad science reporting. In her 2019 book *The Gendered Brain*, neuroscientist Gina Rippon details the "neurotrash" that flooded mainstream media in the late 1990s and early 2000s, when excitement about this technology led to huge overreaches in the media. Reductive conclusions were drawn from the brain scan images that handily aligned with researchers' (and general societal) assumptions. For example, we've all heard of the "left brain" and "right brain" idea: that people who mainly use the left side of their brain are more logical and analytical, while those who mostly use their right brain are more creative. In a 2022 interview, Rippon notes that this is a classic example of neurotrash, spreading the broad-brushstroke idea that the brain is "a 'game of two halves,' when in fact the whole of your brain is working for you the whole of the time."[1]

While fMRI scans have unlocked a wealth of new knowledge about our brains, this knowledge is often disseminated too simplistically. The mainstream media have largely used fMRI images to draw a paint-by-numbers picture of the brain, suggesting that there tends to be a specific "area" of the brain that controls one aspect of your humanity. Along with the "left" and "right" brain, you might hear media chatter about the "reward center" or "pleasure center" in the brain, or even an "empathy circuit." Dividing the brain up into sections in this way reminds me of The Numskulls: a comic strip that has run in the British comic anthology magazine *The Beano* for decades. In The Numskulls, a gang of scrappy little cartoon men operate the bodily functions of a small boy. Brainy, leader of the Numskulls, is of course in charge of the brain.

In the Numskull-ification of neuroscience in popular culture, we tend to believe that there is, for example, a Pleasure Numskull driving our reckless desire for one more drink, or a Clever Numskull who is holding the wheel when we're deep in a Dostoyevsky novel or a crossword puzzle. This makes an innate kind of sense, but it's also a simplification of how the brain works.

Take the concept of "reward" in the brain, for example. This is something we frequently see discussed in the media, as in this 2021 headline: "Listening to music triggers the same reward center in the brain as alcohol and cocaine, study finds."[2] In reality, the "reward center" is not one area of the brain, but a tangled web of neural networks. Research has found that we have slightly different but overlapping areas of activity in the brain related to different kinds of "reward"—for example, listening to music or doing drugs.[3] Without the ability to see brain activity in greater detail than fMRI will allow, it's difficult to make definitive statements about which of these processes are necessary for us to consciously feel a sense of "reward" or pleasure.[4]

In conversations about reward in the brain, we regularly hear about dopamine: the feel-good hormone that we may joke about receiving as a little treat when online shopping or scrolling through TikTok. It's become popular in recent years to talk of giving your brain a "dopamine detox"—starving yourself of social media or other bingeable pleasures as a kind of factory reset of the nervous system. But all this talk of dopamine as the pleasure hormone is reductive. Dopamine can be released not only in rewarding situations, but also in surprising or unpleasant situations like being woken unexpectedly, or even receiving an electric shock.[5] Its function has been shown to be different depending on the situation and brain region that it's released in.[6] Scientists are still working on concretely defining its role in the brain.

In fact, neuroscientists acknowledge that due to the very personal nature of how we each feel a sense of "reward," even defining this in order to study it is a minefield.[7] Some neuroscientists question how helpful it is to connect neural processes to subjective emotional experiences generally—with one prominent researcher who has carried out a great deal of research into the brain's "fear system" writing that he regrets using the term "fear" in his work at all.[8]

All of which is to say, despite the confidence of newspaper headlines that speak of the brain's "anxiety cells" or "generosity spot," neuroscience is a field that contends with big philosophical questions about consciousness, and so is necessarily shrouded with uncertainty and gray areas.[9] This is the backdrop against which scientists have attempted to locate "empathy" in the brain.

First of all, neuroscientists are faced with the Herculean task of defining what empathy even is. Many papers on the subject start with a long-winded explanation of how to define the "empathy" that the particular paper is looking for, whether that's cognitive empathy (often used interchangeably with "Theory of Mind"), affective empathy (or "emotional contagion"), or some other emotional experience entirely, like compassion or sympathy. Take, for example, a 2020 paper on "understanding empathy and its disorders," in which a group of neuroscientists explain the neural mechanisms that they believe are behind a perceived lack of empathy in borderline personality disorder, narcissistic personality disorder, and frontotemporal dementia. The researchers note that empathy is "hard to define or operationalize," and map it on to a complicated web of overlapping brain processes, while also noting that it is impossible to separate "cognitive" and "affective" empathy, neurobiologically speaking. Unable to point to a single impairment shared by all of these neurodivergent people, the researchers double down and commit to identifying and assessing impairments in multiple different brain processes.[10]

Despite many researchers' dedication to finding "empathy" (and a lack of it) in the brain, there has been no groundbreaking piece of research that has definitively done so. Back in the introduction, I quoted the renowned autism researcher Uta Frith, who claims that there is a "GPS"-style device in the brain that has "gone wrong" in the minds of autistic people, leading to a lack of empathy. But no study has shown that autistic people all have the same impairment in their brains. Instead, the research into autistic brains, and the brains of other neurodivergent people who are thought to "lack empathy," has reached diverse conclusions and inspired a lot of debate. Importantly—I sincerely hope that if you take anything away from reading this book, it's this—there is no single device in your brain that controls "empathy." To argue anything otherwise is an oversimplification.

In the past, some have argued that the "Theory of Mind circuit" might be the part of the brain that is "missing" or broken in autistic people. This would mean that autistic people have damage to the parts of their brains that are responsible for ToM—the mind-reading ability that we explored in the previous chapter. Multiple parts of the brain have been nominated as potentially being the Mind-Reading Numskull, yet brain imaging studies have so far failed to identify a single brain mechanism that controls this ability.[11] This makes it highly unlikely that autistic people are missing or impaired in this specific mechanism, since it doesn't seem to exist.

While brain imaging has failed to identify a single location of ToM in the brain, it has pointed to multiple areas that are thought to be important for cognitive empathy.

Still, the relationship between the colorful, clean image of an fMRI scan and the lived, embodied reality of the brain are unclear. This has been demonstrated in studies carried out with people who have suffered brain damage, which do not always yield the results you might expect to see. In 2004, Frith and a team of fellow researchers carried out tests on a patient who had suffered a stroke that had led to significant damage in the medial frontal cortex, an area thought to be critical for ToM. Yet the patient was found to score in the "normal" ranges on most of the ToM tests she was given. The bemused scientists concluded that there were limits to what we can learn about brain anatomy from images of blood flow in the brain.[12] These images are like surveillance photographs taken from high above the earth: We can't see what is happening on the street level. We can't plug into what is happening deep down in our neural pathways where activity unfolds beyond our reach and at the speed of electricity.

In the early 2000s, excitement surrounded another discovery that was purported to identify empathy in the brain. "Mirror neurons" had first been observed by Italian neuroscientist Giacomo Rizzolatti and colleagues at the University of Parma in the early 1990s. Rizzolatti's team were setting out to study the neurons that fire in macaque monkeys' brains when they performed certain tasks, such as grasping a peanut. The researchers were surprised to discover, in a happy accident, that the same neurons fired in the monkeys' brains when they *watched* the researcher grasping a peanut, as when they grasped a peanut themselves.

Further research showed that the monkeys' motor neurons would not only light up in response to watching other monkeys and people do things, but that they would do this with alarming specificity. If a researcher popped a peanut into their mouth in view of a monkey, the same neurons would fire in the monkey's brain as would fire if the monkey had popped a peanut into their own mouth.[13] The researchers dubbed their discovery "mirror neurons."

This research was carried out by attaching electrodes directly to the monkeys' brains, which was a terrible time for the monkeys. For obvious reasons, this research has never been replicated with humans. However, neuroscientists set about trying to identify the existence of a similar mirror neuron system in humans. Most of this research has been carried out with fMRI imaging, which—although unable to capture the precision of individual neurons—has shown that similar areas of the brain are activated when people watch one another perform certain tasks. It's worth taking these findings with a healthy pinch of salt. Brain imaging shows us that, in humans, the part of the brain associated with eating a peanut, for example, may light up when you watch someone else eat a peanut. But while the research on monkeys showed that this was down to the exact same neurons firing, with imaging human brains, we can observe only an area of around three square millimeters—an area that may contain millions of individual neurons.[14]

Empathy is embodied

Despite a lack of concrete evidence that mirror neurons exist in human brains in the same way that they do in macaque brains—and no concrete explanation for exactly what function mirror neurons perform—it has been suggested that they might be critical to empathy. In the early 2000s, multiple researchers argued that these mystical mirror neurons might have something to do with a subconscious, innate form of empathy—and that "faulty" mirror neurons might therefore be the key to understanding autism.[15] In 2005 and 2006, two studies claimed to show that autistic people had abnormal mirror neuron activity. These results were breathlessly reported in *The New York Times* as being a crucial step in explaining what autism really is. The author of the 2006 study, Mirella Dapretto, was quoted in the *Times* as saying that mirror neurons were not involved in the process of consciously imagining yourself in another's place, but in "really feeling what another person is feeling,"[16] or affective empathy. But mirror neurons have also been linked to our capacity for Theory of Mind, cognitive empathy, and even the ability to learn language. All this, despite the fact that, as neuroscientist Gregory Hickock points out, "the species that has been shown to possess mirror neurons [macaque monkeys] does not, to our knowledge, possess any of these higher-order cognitive processes, and the species that possesses the higher-order cognitive processes [humans], has not been shown conclusively to possess mirror neurons."[17]

Autistic people are believed to have a faulty mirror

neuron system because autistic children have been shown to fail "mirroring" imitation tests. That is, when a researcher performs an action such as pulling a silly facial expression, autistic children are less likely to spontaneously copy that expression than non-autistic children. If we assume that mirror neurons have a role to play in imitation, researchers argued, then a broken mirror neuron system might be the key to explaining the social problems that autistic people have. Hence, the "broken mirror" theory of autism.

In a 2008 paper, cognitive neuroscientists Victoria Southgate and Antonia Hamilton detail several major problems with this theory.[18] First of all, they point out, macaque monkeys do not imitate one another. That's already a pretty major nail in the coffin for the broken mirror theory. Even if we're not extrapolating wildly about the implications of a mirror neuron system for empathizing and relationship-building, and instead only zeroing in on the basic function of "monkey see, monkey do," there is still no evidence that the macaque monkeys—as Hickock notes, the only species that has been proven to definitely possess mirror neurons—actually *do* see, and *do* do.

What's more, autistic children's lack of imitation is not necessarily a sign of an inability to imitate. For example, Southgate and Hamilton note that autistic children have been shown to perform better on imitation tasks when they are explicitly instructed to imitate the researchers. Without this instruction, autistic children simply don't repeat the meaningless facial expressions and gestures of the researchers. (Honestly, I can relate.) Southgate and Hamilton note that this finding could be the result of the children not reading social cues in the same way as non-autistic children—for instance, because they tend to avoid looking directly at people's faces—rather than a sign of a missing component of the brain that would instruct the children to imitate. Once again, we can't reduce the tangled web of brain processes—and how these complicated processes relate to our embodied, social reality—down to individual Numskulls.

Since the broken mirror theory, researchers have looked for other areas of the brain that might relate to autistic differences in empathy. One contender is the amygdala—the tiny almond-shaped part of the brain that has been linked to the feeling of fear and other strong emotions. But with some studies finding a link between autism and a larger-than-average amygdala, and other studies finding the reverse, the conclusion remains unclear.[19] Some studies have suggested that autistic people have lower levels of the hormone oxytocin[20]—commonly described as the "love hormone." Others have investigated how autistic people's differences in sensory processing might influence how we relate to other people and how we empathize.[21]

The present picture of what we know about empathy in the brain is less like a Numskulls comic strip, and more like an impressionistic painting. We now know that there are areas of the brain that are involved in empathy-related processes: language, emotion, and social relationships. The inferior frontal gyrus, the inferior parietal lobule, the ventromedial prefrontal cortex, the temporoparietal junction, and the medial temporal lobe have all been invoked as important parts of the brain for empathizing.[22] Behavioral differences in developmental disorders like autism have been attributed to the "mirror" network (parietal and prefrontal regions), the amygdala network (the amygdala and orbitofrontal regions), the "mentalizing" network (the medial prefrontal and superior temporal regions), and the "empathy" network (insula and amygdala regions).[23] All of those regions listed together might feel like little more than a word salad, but the overall picture is that there is no one specific region of the brain that controls what we call "empathy."

In the Decade of the Brain, we were taught that examining pictures of our brains could give us answers to human nature. The truth is, of course, much more complicated. Brains are not easily divided into distinct areas that control distinct behaviors, and similarly, people are not reducible to their brains. We are whole selves that are made up of bio-psycho-social elements: We are as complex as our environments. But this narrative is not catchy enough to derail popular narratives about the brain—particularly those that align with the deeply held biases we already have that can be used to uphold society's status quo. Biological determinism is a hell of a drug, and it's fueled the unstoppable rise of one of the most culturally entrenched ideas about empathy in the brain: the gendered idea that women are biologically "wired" for empathy, and men are not.

Empathy and the "male brain"

Biological determinism is the idea that our biology influences the society we create, rather than the other way around—in other words, nature triumphs over nurture. One classic example is the pervasive idea that women are biologically predisposed to be "maternal," and so take on the primary caregiving responsibilities for children, whereas recent research shows that men also experience changes in their bodies and brains that prime them for caregiving when they become parents.[24] In the early 2000s, Simon Baron-Cohen, the researcher behind the Theory of Mind model of autism, made his own contribution to the genre. In his 2003 book *The Essential Difference*, Baron-Cohen wrote two sentences that would come to shape public discourse about gender and the brain for years to come. "The female brain is predominantly hard-wired for empathy," he declared. "The male brain is predominantly hard-wired for understanding and building systems."[25]

These statements reinforce what Baron-Cohen named the empathizing-systemizing (or E-S) theory of human brains, which suggests that we all exist along the spectrum of a distinct gender binary: Our brains are hardwired either to understand other people, or to understand "systems." Once again, in this framing, we encounter the language of "wiring," that unshakable computer metaphor of the human mind.

The distinction that Baron-Cohen draws between E-type (or "female") and S-type (or "male") brains goes far beyond whether you're a good listener. In fact, he associates a whole slew of potential activities and interests with either type of brain. He writes:

"Those with the male brain tend to spend hours happily engaged in car or motorbike maintenance, small-plane piloting, sailing, bird- or train-spotting, mathematics, tweaking their sound systems, or busy with computer games and programming, DIY or photography. Those with the female brain tend to prefer to spend their time engaged in coffee mornings or having supper with friends, advising them on relationship problems, or caring for people or pets, or working for volunteer phone-lines listening to depressed, hurt, needy or even suicidal anonymous callers."[26]

Most of us supposedly exist somewhere along this spectrum. But Baron-Cohen proposed that autistic people have an "extreme" example of an S-type or male brain. This would mean that the fundamental identifying feature of autism is a propensity for "systemizing," and a lack of "empathizing," and that we autistic people are biologically predisposed to prefer train-spotting and small-plane piloting to caring for pets or talking to our friends.

The E-S theory is an extremely clear-cut example of a

neuroscientific theory that has caught the public imagination by virtue of how neatly it aligns with our pre-existing social norms, and in fact suggests that those norms are biological realities. Baron-Cohen frames his theory in terms of benign hobbies, like tinkering with motorbikes, suggesting that men and women simply have different pastimes. But the ramifications of what he is suggesting run much deeper, as these interests and skills are valued differently by society. This theory appears to confirm that women are programmed to be interested in things that are not respected or seen as difficult in our capitalist society—such as hosting a coffee morning, or offering emotional support—while men have a built-in knack for technology and logic, pursuits that are characterized as more serious. How convenient it is to have a scientific theory that reifies our existing gender roles, by confirming that men are just *better* at the kind of work that is highly regarded and paid in our society, while women are hardwired to do the empathetic care work and emotional labor that is invisible and unrewarded.

It also aligns neatly with how autism is characterized in the popular imagination. At the time of coining the term "extreme male brain," diagnosis of "high-functioning" autistic boys outnumbered girls by a ratio of about 10:1.[27] In 2024, the National Autistic Society claimed that the most current estimate is a ratio of 3:1.[28] The tide is slowly turning, but the stereotypical idea of what it means to be autistic still lingers. It is viewed—as it was labeled by

Baron-Cohen in a 2005 *New York Times* article—as a "male condition."[29] The rise of the extreme male brain theory coincided with an emerging "geek masculinity" archetype that itself is linked to autism.[30] In 2001, *Wired* published an article titled "The Geek Syndrome" exploring an "epidemic" of autism in Silicon Valley.[31] It doesn't feel like a big leap, from this deeply embedded social stereotype, to suggest that male brains are more computer-like than female, and that autistic brains are the most computer-like (and hence the most male) of all.

Baron-Cohen's theory has been skewered by experts, including psychologist Cordelia Fine (who labeled it "neurosexism") and neuroscientist Gina Rippon, who have both written about the ways in which the theory unquestioningly replicates and perpetuates sexist ideas. In Cordelia Fine's 2010 book *Delusions of Gender*, she sarcastically summarizes popular culture's attitude toward "male" and "female" brains in this way: "If you want the answer to persisting gender inequalities, stop peering suspiciously at society and take a look right over here, please, at this brain scan."[32] Both Fine and Rippon have detailed the ways in which the E-S theory falsely perpetuates the idea that our brains influence society, rather than the other way around: The plasticity of our brains means that they respond to our experiences.

When I ask scientist and author Camilla Pang about the extreme male brain theory, I can hear the frustration in her voice. Camilla is a computational biologist who has also written multiple books about the experience of being autistic and having ADHD. I tell her that I'm curious about her thoughts on this theory, both as a scientist and as a fellow neurodivergent person. "I think the extreme male brain theory is very reductionist," she says, not skipping a beat. She's talking to me on the phone over the sound of whooshing wind while walking her dog, Wendy. "It's really biased toward white, male experiences. And it actually ignores the fact that in order to be systematic, you have to have a healthy amount of both rationality and empathy. They're not a zero sum!"

She notes that the big thing missing from the theory is any sense of social context: Who gets to be seen as "empathetic," and who gets to be seen as "systematic"? "What this theory doesn't take into account is the impact of masking," Camilla muses. "I'm female, and I'm more likely to mask when someone is suspicious of me. I know a lot of neurodivergent people of color, and they mask because they feel like society is already suspicious of them. You already feel like you're 'wrong.'" So-called hardwired traits of "empathy" may in fact be survival instincts, as women and other marginalized people don a people-pleasing mask to get by in an unequal society. Saying that this is a biological fact of our brains erases the social and cultural nuances of this behavior. Or as Camilla puts it, this theory "not only minimizes the experiences of those that have been marginalized, but it generalizes."

Camilla herself, with a career that straddles the arts and

sciences, is a living, breathing illustration of how real life doesn't fit neatly into the E-S binary: having a lot of one doesn't automatically mean you have less of the other. Or, in her own words, "I am both a rational and irrational person—I'm emotional, and I'm logical. It's not about being rational or emotional, or systemizing or empathetic, it's about the social permission that enables you to be either. For women that's different, and for people of different races that's different." In Camilla's career, her refusal to fit neatly into one box has led online trolls to email her suggesting that her autism diagnosis must not be real, as she is able to write creatively. She shrugs this off: "It's a show of ignorance when someone stereotypes you."

Baron-Cohen claims that his theory is apolitical. In fact, in 2010, he accused his critic, Cordelia Fine, of "the mistaken blurring of science with politics." Describing her work as a "polemic," he concludes that "fusing science with politics is, in my view, unfounded."[33] Baron-Cohen's argument takes a binary view of science versus politics, or biology versus society. Biology cannot be questioned, he argues: It is irrefutable fact, and exists separately to our social and political reality. It is this black-and-white way of thinking that is, itself, one of the core problems with the E-S theory. Must something be *either* scientific or political, *either* biological or social, *either* male or female, *either* systemizing or empathizing—can it not be both?

Of course, creating a theory that claims that gender differences—differences that have a material, lived effect in our society, impacting everything from how much you get paid to how likely you are to be assaulted or murdered—are biologically hardwired is not a politically neutral act. However, if we take Baron-Cohen's own advice and try to remove politics from our critique of the extreme male brain theory of empathy, there are still plenty of issues with the idea. For one thing, it has not been scientifically proven, and so remains an idea, not a fact. There are three main ways that the extreme male brain theory has been tested: studies that explore the effect of exposure to testosterone in the womb on developing children, brain imaging tests that look at the differences between male and female brains, and self-report questionnaires that measure people's "systemizing" and "empathizing" traits. In all three of these areas, there have been studies that support the theory, and studies that flout it.

It has been speculated that exposure to higher levels of testosterone in the womb could lead to increased chances that a baby will later be diagnosed with autism, and studies from Baron-Cohen's lab have found connections between fetal testosterone and the development of "male" brains.[34] But there has been a lack of notable replication of results supporting the extreme male brain theory from outside of Baron-Cohen's own research center.[35] One significant, widely cited 2016 paper found no relationship at all between fetal testosterone and autistic traits.[36]

So, we return to our faithful brain images: What can these tell us about "male" and "female" brains? The picture is unclear. One small 2012 study (looking at the brains of just fifteen men and thirteen women) found that there were fewer differences between the brains of autistic men and women than between their neurotypical counterparts.[37] But a major 2017 brain imaging study that suggested that autistic women had more "male" brains than non-autistic women was retracted in 2019, after researchers found that their results had been skewed by a statistical error.[38]

One of the main sources of support for the theory again came from Baron-Cohen's own research lab, in 2018. As part of a Channel 4 TV show called *Are You Autistic?*, over six hundred thousand people, including 36,648 autistic people, volunteered to take a series of questionnaires assessing where they fall on the E-S scale. The results supported the E-S theory, with males tending to be S-type, women tending more toward E-type, and autistic people showing more muted gender differences than the rest of the population.[39] While these results support the theory that women and men tend on average toward either "empathizing" or "systemizing" based on their gender, it is questionable to attribute this difference to "hardwiring" in the brain, given that the results come from self-report questionnaires. As Gina Rippon writes of self-report measures in *The Gendered Brain*, they are "reliant on people's own opinions of what they (or their children) are like."[40]

The participants responded to a questionnaire named the Empathy Quotient, devised by Simon Baron-Cohen and Sally Wheelwright in 2004. It comprises sixty questions, forty of which are designed to determine how "empathetic" the respondent is. (The other twenty are decoys, designed only to distract the participant from the purpose of the questionnaire.) The questions measure both cognitive and affective empathy traits, though the researchers have argued that low scores on the E-Q are more likely to be a result of "difficulties primarily with cognitive empathy (or theory of mind), rather than all components of empathy."[41]

If you ask me, the E-Q's questions aren't assessing empathy at all. Instead, they're assessing how much you value social behavior, and more importantly, whether you're capable of what's considered "normal" social behavior. For example, take the very first question on the test. The E-Q presents its questions as statements, with which the respondent must "definitely agree," "slightly agree," and so on. The first statement posed is: "I can easily tell if someone else wants to enter a conversation."

What is this question looking for? It could be identifying the ability to attribute mental states to others: to know that other people might want to join a conversation that you're part of, and to recognize when someone is feeling that way ("I can easily imagine the perspective of the person who is standing outside the conversation I'm having and can see my own rudeness through their eyes"). It may be looking for an affective sensitivity, or even a sense of vigilance toward the feelings of others in social situations

("I can easily sense the air of a room turning dark and the space feeling smaller when somebody is waiting with frustration to speak"). It could be said to be measuring social tact or politeness ("I can easily bring others seamlessly into my conversations, remember everyone's names at parties, and never run out of fun cocktail hour conversation topics").

Mostly, the question encourages you to consider how well you fit in at parties. I'm immediately struck by the question's invitation to imagine yourself as part of the in-crowd, either benevolently inviting the socially anxious person to speak, or ignoring them. What if you identify far more with the introvert in this scenario, chewing their words in silence, than with the person already having a conversation?

The idea that this question is a measure of empathy has clear flaws. How you answer a question like this might have much more to do with your role in society and ease in social situations than how you "empathize." Women may, on average, score higher on the E-Q because they've been raised to hone their empathizing skills over and above their systemizing skills, and because they know that women are "supposed" to have these skills. When we answer questions about ourselves, we all have our society and culture looking over our shoulders. To draw conclusions from such self-reporting about the essential nature of our "female brains" is dangerous.

It's also worth interrogating who is left out of this

research. In this study of six hundred thousand people, for example, the researchers note that they excluded those who are minimally speaking or nonspeaking, and those with intellectual disabilities.[42] Given that estimates of the number of minimally speaking or nonspeaking autistic people hover around 25 percent of the autistic population,[43] and that people with learning disabilities are twenty-two times more likely to be diagnosed autistic than those without,[44] this is a huge gap in the research. We have to consider, also, the general historical bias of autism research toward white, middle class, English-speaking boys, and how that has also skewed the data that we have toward the experiences of those specific demographics.

The "extreme male brain" theory is damaging for autistic people, as it perpetuates the unfeeling, robotic stereotype of autism, and fails to recognize the diversity in autistic people. But the ramifications of this theory go far beyond the autistic community. We need to reject biological determinist narratives about the brain as we work toward a fairer, more just society. Accepting that men are coded for "systemizing" and women are coded for "empathizing" is reductive. It cages us in binary roles: males and females, thinkers and feelers. It assumes that only women are capable of "soft skills" like empathy, and that the biology of men blunts their ability to love and care for others. There is nothing expansive about this way of thinking. It doesn't give us any room to change, or to grow as people.

Recent research into neuroplasticity—the "plastic,"

changeable nature of our brains—shows that there is plenty of reason to doubt that your ability to empathize is "hardwired." Researchers in the relatively new field of social neuroscience have been examining how the "empathetic" brain responses seen in fMRI scans are modulated by various external factors. For example, you might empathize more with people that you relate to more (such as someone on your football team, rather than your opponent), or people that you deem to be demonstrating "fair" behavior.[45] It has also been demonstrated that taking action to change your empathetic responses—for example, by practicing loving kindness meditation,[46] or spending more time with people of different races and cultures—can change the imaging results observed in your brain.[47]

Given the complex interrelatedness of empathy processes in the brain, and the multiple parts of the brain that are said to play a role in empathizing, we have to take results of studies like these with a healthy dose of skepticism. The kind of "empathy" being shown by an area of the brain lighting up in an fMRI scanner is likely to be just one star in a galaxy of thinking and feeling. But findings like these reveal that your brain and its capacity for empathy are malleable. You are not on autopilot, being driven by the Numskulls in your mind. You can make adjustments in your life that can literally change how your brain responds to other people. Any of us can learn to think and feel differently. We are not static objects; we are beings that live and evolve.

Empathy as a sense

Of course, some biological differences *do* influence the ways in which we empathize; society isn't the only thing that matters. Like everything else, these two realities are not zero-sum. While there is no "empathy device" that's been located in the brain, emerging neuroscientific studies about neurodivergent bodyminds have provided valuable new perspectives on how empathy is expressed and experienced by us all. Many of these theories sketch out empathy as a sensory, full-body experience, and highlight how differences in sensory processing may impact the ways in which we connect with others.

Our understanding of autistic brains is still in its infancy. As the "Autistic Neuroscientist" puts it in a YouTube short video, "Even the 'experts' are still learning."[48] The Autistic Neuroscientist is Hari Srinivasan, a PhD neuroscience student at Vanderbilt University in Tennessee and board member of the Autistic Self Advocacy Network (ASAN). His PhD research, he tells me over email, is driven by his advocacy and his desire to "seek research that is meaningful which (hopefully) will lead to translatable solutions." Hari is specifically working in the realm of sensory neuroscience, looking at peripersonal space and the related concept of embodied cognition—that is, how we perceive our bodies as existing in space, and the role our bodies play in shaping our inner worlds. Hari is hoping that his research into the embodied experiences of autistic people will lead to tech solutions that can provide practical support in the future.

Hearing about Hari's work is exciting to me, as a psychotherapist and as an autistic person, for two reasons. Firstly, because it looks to create actual, real-world solutions to improve accessibility, rather than seeking to pathologize or stigmatize autistic people. And secondly, because it looks at the experience of the entire bodymind, rather than perpetuating the myth of mind–body dualism. Sensory neuroscience illuminates the complexity of our whole bodies as thinking, feeling systems. We are constantly receiving information from the outside world, not as data being fed into a computer, but as salt on our tongues, air on our skin, twisting sensations in our guts.

One of the most commonly cited theories about the sensory worlds of autistic people is the Intense World Theory, proposed by the South African and German neuroscientist couple Henry and Kamila Markram. The couple were inspired in their research by the experiences of Henry's son, a nonspeaking autistic man. The essential idea behind their theory is that, while autism research in the past has focused on finding the under-responsive or malfunctioning parts of autistic brains, it may be possible that the autistic brain is actually *hyper*-responsive and *hyper*-functioning. This would mean that we process things much more intensely than the average person, and so things that may not be overwhelming for non-autistic people—like a bad smell, or the emotional intricacies of a social situation—may be incapacitating for us.[49] By way of illustration, consider comedian Fern Brady's description in her memoir, *Strong Female Character*, of a manicurist cutting her nails too short, leaving her with "the sensation that my fingertips are raw" and causing an autistic meltdown that left her unable to function.[50]

Avoiding the relentless sensory onslaught of the Intense World may lead autistic people to retreat into their minds, or stick to the safe rigidity of a routine. It's not hard to see how this could account for what's perceived as a "lack of empathy." When social and sensory information is overwhelming, it makes sense to deaden your senses toward it. Trying to have a conversation in a loud bar, for example, can be difficult for anyone. For an autistic person, it can be debilitating. It might be impossible to control our tone, facial expressions, or even to speak at all, while being bombarded with noise and lights that are sending our sensitive bodies into a fight-or-flight response. All autistic people are different, but the Intense World Theory is one that chimes closely with my experiences. The closer I am to overwhelm—whether it's from the fluorescent lights in an office, unpredictable social interactions, burnout, or all of the above—the "more autistic" I feel and behave.

Offices in particular have always been a site of social difficulty for me, not only due to the general fatigue of sensory overwhelm, but because of the way my mind stumbles over switching tasks. Part of my autistic experience is that I find myself hyper-focusing, or entering what might be called a "flow state" when I'm interested in something. Often, when I'm writing or otherwise deep in a task, it's as though my other senses dim. Someone could be calling my name from centimeters away, and I wouldn't hear. Sometimes I get absorbed in social interactions, too. A date once teased me for being so focused on our flirtatious conversation on the London Overground that I failed to notice a drunk man loudly vomiting right behind us. This hyper-focus can be a boon to empathy—I'd argue that it's part of what makes me a good therapist—but it can also impede my expression of empathy in day-to-day situations, where I might seem aloof, brusque, or inattentive.

A prominent theory about this aspect of autistic bodyminds is "monotropism," a brainchild of the late autistic academic Dinah Murray. Murray's big idea was that the key way in which autistic minds differ from non-autistic minds is in how they pay attention. Autistic people tend to zero in on one thing at a time: If there's a task, we are fully absorbed in it. If there's a conversation happening, we need our full mental power to take part. If there are two things happening at once (say, a conversation to maintain, and the overwhelming sound of a lorry reversing outside), we may become overwhelmed. In Murray's view, this monotropism is behind both our strengths (an ability to intensely hyper-focus on the things we find interesting) and our disability (struggling to cope with multiple sources of stimulation or information at once).

In her seminal 2005 paper on the subject, Murray and

her fellow researchers explained how monotropism might underscore the social problems observed in autistic people. "In a monotropic child, recognition of the existence of others will occur only in so far as other people are engaged with fulfilling the interests which preoccupy that child. Otherwise the existence of other people, like the existence of everything outside the tightly focused monotropic attention tunnel, may not impinge at all."[51] In practice, this may look like an autistic person intentionally blanking you, being rude, or caring only for themselves, when in actual fact, they simply have a limited amount of attention to pay. It's easy to imagine how the autistic child, fixated on the sensation of rocking backward and forward, or on the sound of the spinning wheels of their toy car, might seem uninterested or disengaged when an adult tries to talk to them or play with them.* This disconnection may not be a result of the self-absorption or lack of empathy that researchers have suggested in the past, but a total immersion in their own sensory world (the breeze on their cheeks as they sway back and forth, the gliding *whoosh* of small plastic wheels).

Another way in which autistic sensory processing might account for differences in expressing empathy is in our experience of our own inner worlds. Many autistic people report having difficulty with "interoception"—the sense

---

* This kind of self-stimulatory behavior is often described with the neologism "stimming."

that allows us to notice how we're feeling inside our bodies. Sometimes called the "hidden sense,"[52] interoception is how you notice internal physical sensations—like hunger or needing to go to the bathroom—and also emotional states, like the first embers of anger. Autistic people broadly have a lower interoceptive awareness.[53] In other words, we feel a chronic disconnection from what's going on inside our bodyminds, whether that's a need to drink water or a need to scream.

How this manifests for many autistic people is in something called "alexithymia"—a pseudo-diagnostic label for not being able to easily recognize or name your own emotions. Around half of autistic people are thought to have some level of alexithymia.[54] There's a clear connection between difficulty interpreting your own emotional state and difficulty relating to others. Researchers in 2010 found that levels of "empathy" were more likely to be affected by alexithymia than autism. In the study, scientists used fMRI imaging to look at "empathic brain responses" in people who were observing others in pain, and found that both autistic and non-autistic people showed differences in this kind of empathy in relation to their self-reported level of alexithymia—not according to whether they were autistic.[55]

A disclaimer: I still don't believe that these brain scans can wholly represent "empathy" as a multi-faceted process—but they can offer useful insights. As a psychotherapist, it makes sense to me that not feeling attuned to your own emotions would make it harder to attune to the emotions of others. It also makes sense that growing up autistic in a neuronormative world might cause you to feel some detachment from your inner emotional life. This is not because of an built-in fault in the brain, but because of trauma. Constantly being invalidated or misunderstood may lead you to feel that it's not safe to trust nor even fully feel your body's signals.

This is not only significant for autistic people. Alexithymia is commonly reported by those who have experienced trauma. Significantly, 42 percent of those diagnosed with PTSD are estimated to exhibit alexithymia, and struggle to identify their own emotions.[56] Anyone who has been traumatized in childhood may find that their sensory world is impacted more generally, with emerging research finding a strong correlation between adverse experiences early in life and sensory processing difficulties later on.[57] Again and again in my work, I see how trauma's impact causes ruptures and barriers in our relationships and ability to connect with one another. Healing this is a process that involves not just the mind, but the whole body.

Trauma and empathy

The idea that trauma lives in our bodies has been popularized in the Western world in the last ten years by the omnipresent book on the subject, *The Body Keeps the Score*, by Dutch psychiatrist Bessel van der Kolk. Though this book's extended time on *The New York Times* bestseller list has widely disseminated the idea that our bodies store memories of trauma, this is not a new concept. Trauma specialist Babette Rothschild wrote about the psychopathology of trauma in 2000, in a book titled *The Body Remembers*, and renowned psychologist Alice Miller wrote about the lasting physical symptoms for victims of child abuse in her book *The Body Never Lies* in 2004. Psychotherapist Resmaa Menakem has expanded on this idea by exploring how the trauma of living under white supremacy impacts the bodies of all Americans, and how it can be healed in his groundbreaking book *My Grandmother's Hands*.

Though "trauma" has become something of a buzzword in the 2020s, the development of the concept of trauma and how to treat it in the Western world spans the last several decades, roughly beginning with the end of World War II. My own work as a psychotherapist is hugely influenced by the feminist psychiatrist Judith Herman, who wrote the seminal book *Trauma and Recovery* in 1992. She described three crucial stages to recovery from trauma, the first being the need to feel a sense of safety in your body. It is only once you achieve this that you can move on to the next stages of trauma recovery: remembering and mourning the traumatic incident, and integrating your trauma into your sense of self.[58] Herman and the other trauma specialists have this in common: They emphasize the

Empathy is embodied

importance of feeling safe before any work can be done. Similarly, it is only once we feel calm and rooted in ourselves that we can meaningfully connect with others. When the internal alarm systems of our bodies are going off, how can we hear the voices of others over the noise?

This idea crops up in polyvagal theory, a theory about nervous systems proposed by psychologist Dr. Stephen Porges in 2009.[59] Porges suggests that we generally exist in three nervous states: a safe and social state, known as "ventral vagal"; a hypervigilant, fight-or-flight state, known as "sympathetic vagal"; and a shutdown, exhausted state, or "dorsal vagal." Porges was influenced by his work with autistic children, who, he observed, were much more socially skilled when they were in their "ventral vagal" state, and showed more autistic traits when they were tipped into "sympathetic vagal" or "dorsal vagal."[60]

Though this theory has been strongly criticized[61] and said to oversimplify human biology, its central idea makes an innate kind of sense to me, in the same way as the Intense World Theory: I'm least likely to be able to make eye contact or small talk when I'm in fight-or-flight mode. When I feel grounded, I'm more able to express empathy. I use somatic exercises—like touching my chest or touching the ground—and deep breathing to center myself before sessions with clients. It might look a bit strange if a colleague were to walk into my therapy room and catch me there, sighing alone into the carpet, but it brings me a sense of peacefulness that makes for better listening.

As a talking therapist, my sessions inevitably center around speech. But some therapists work more directly with the body to tackle trauma. T. Aisha Edwards, a therapist based near Portland, Oregon, originally trained as a talking therapist, but now also uses touch- and movement-based interventions with clients, such as rhythmic rocking. Aisha's practice draws on Western and Eastern influences, mixing traditional Chinese medicine and African shamanic healing with EMDR therapy, which uses eye movements and other stimuli, like gentle tapping, to help process traumatic memories. Developmental trauma is stored in our bodies, and so it makes sense that processing it can be a bodily experience. With a laugh, xey describe thoughts and speech as "the end of a train that's left the station a long time ago."*

To Aisha, empathy is "entirely energetic." Xey give an example that we can all recognize: "You know what it's like when you walk into a room where something awkward has happened, or where people were fighting, and the room feels charged? When people say the phrase 'read the room,' that's what they're talking about!" For many traumatized people, being able to pick up on and respond to these signals may not be easy. Or, as Aisha puts it to me, our bodies are often communicating a message of *not safe, not safe, not safe*. Living with this sense of brittle hypervigilance can create the appearance of a "lack of empathy," as our

---

* Aisha uses the gender-neutral pronouns xey/xem/xer.

Empathy is embodied

defenses stop us from connecting with one another. "It's very hard to have a sense of togetherness when I feel threatened," says Aisha.

Part of training as a therapist, for me, meant trying to unpack how trauma showed up in my own bodymind, and impacted my own ability to feel close to others. This was not something that could be learned from textbooks. It had to be felt. In my first year of training, my tutors would consistently tell me in their feedback that I must learn to prioritize "being, not doing." Disgruntled, I would ask them to clarify what they meant. I'm a lifelong overthinker, used to researching and planning and working out the best course of action. I had returned to higher education prepared to research and theorize my way toward academic success, only to find myself stumped by this experiential approach. The concept of simply *being* was alien to me.

As a trainee counselor, I was supervised in my client work by a tutor, Kara, who was herself an art therapist. Supervision is a process of reflection and accountability, where therapists like myself meet with other, usually more experienced therapists to discuss our client work and make sure we're doing the best we can to support people. Kara was a fan of using creative methods in her work, and so on more than one occasion, I found myself in supervision wielding a paintbrush and being asked to identify the "color" of what I was feeling.

It was difficult for me to put aside my familiar defense mechanism of intellectualizing and embrace this more instinctive way of doing things. One warm summer's evening, in the stuffy office where we met for our fortnightly supervision, I found myself frozen with discomfort by one of Kara's characteristically kooky prompts. As I was sharing my experience with a client I was struggling to relate to, Kara stopped me, and asked me to move across the office to sit in a different chair.

"When you sit in this chair," she instructed, "you will, as if by magic, transform into this client. You will embody them, and show me through movement what it's like to be them."

I glared at the empty chair sitting across from us and felt my nerves prickle. Kara sensed my hesitation and immediately recognized—correctly—that I was mentally planning what I would do once I sat in the chair.

"Don't think about it," she admonished. "Just do it."

I sat in the chair, my limbs rigid with fear, embarrassment, and anger. How could this be helpful? Why couldn't she just *tell me what to do*?

After a few tense beats of silence, with the heat of Kara's gaze on me, my hand flew to my forehead in frustration, and I exclaimed through almost-gritted teeth, "I just can't get out of my head!"

I felt that I had failed the exercise, and I expected Kara to be stern. Instead, when I lowered my hand from its defensive position across my face, I was surprised to see her smiling.

"This is something you can use," she said.

Empathy is embodied

She was right. Those feelings of tension, anger, and fear were all helpful. In my tightly wound defensiveness, in that chair, I had channeled something of my client's experience: their difficulty with feeling rather than thinking, their constant need to get things "right" rather than embrace the messiness and pain of life. I softened as I realized that these feelings were the whole point. And I was left with some insight about myself, too: My own terror in the face of acting on my instincts was also causing me to have difficulty connecting with this client on a deeper level. I was meeting them intellectually, not emotionally, and so I was getting stuck in loops of rumination with them. I realized that becoming a better therapist was going to mean going deeper into my own emotional world. This is what is meant by "being, not doing." Being truly present in the moment can be more healing than rushing to find a solution, even if that moment feels powerfully uncomfortable to sit with.

The following week, in the counseling room with my client, I practiced being more in tune with my own bodily instincts. My anxious and analytical client was in the middle of a long explanation of all the reasons why a romantic relationship would be too complicated and time-consuming for her to maintain, and at the end of the day, she was happier alone. Though she had clearly put a lot of thought into constructing this argument, and she was making it passionately, as she was speaking, I felt what I could describe only as an iron-weighted sadness drop through me, into the pit of my stomach.

Don't do. Just be.

I abandoned the response to my client's story I'd been carefully mentally scripting, and jumped in to say, "I just felt immensely sad when you said that you're happier alone. I'm wondering, is part of you feeling sad, too?"

My client began to cry, for the first time in our work together. Naming her inadmissible sadness had given it permission to come into the room. For the first time, I felt truly connected to her. Now, deep inside the melancholic fog together, we could begin to look for a way out.

Sometimes, the most powerful expression of empathy is to follow these momentary instincts. It's noticing what you feel in your body, what energy you're sensing in the space between you and another person, and responding to that without stopping to censor or second-guess yourself. All of us may find it harder to be alive to these signals, or to respond to them, when we are feeling threatened—when our bodies are vibrating to the pulse of *not safe, not safe, not safe*. Recognizing that our trauma responses can get in the way of our empathy can also help us to have more self-compassion in those moments that we fail. Our missed connections are not due to a fault in our programming. They're part of being a wounded, imperfect human.

Traditional narratives about empathy tell us that it is something that our brains are "wired" for. But what is wiring without connection? Electricity travels through a wire only when a circuit is completed; when an object is plugged

Empathy is embodied

into something else. Similarly, empathy is not a process contained entirely within the closed system of the brain. Your brain is one part of the ecosystem of your body; your body, one part of the ecosystem of society, culture, relationships, the natural environment. We are natural beings, not machines. But maybe, in a sense, we are conductive metals, raw and permeable, the world's intense voltage constantly flowing through us.

4

Empathy is amoral

Empathy is not inherently good. It is not necessary to feel empathy to do good things; nor is it necessary to lack it to be cruel. Though simple, this idea is fairly taboo. But all feelings, including empathy, are morally neutral. I encourage my clients to let go of moral judgments surrounding their emotions all the time; perhaps when they're angry at a parent who has passed away, for example, or being cut into pieces by grief over a short-term relationship. Many of us find ourselves caught up in a spiral about what we "should" feel, berating ourselves for the feelings we deem to be "bad." But feelings are just feelings: All of us harbor ugly and obscene emotions from time to time. It is the actions that spring from our feelings, and the ways in which we impact others, that have a moral significance.

In his provocatively titled 2016 polemic *Against Empathy*, the psychologist Paul Bloom challenges the commonly repeated refrain that a lack of empathy is at the heart of a myriad of society's evils. He draws on classic philosophical ideas to make his point, including an idea from the Chinese philosopher Mencius: If you walk past a child drowning in a lake, the morally right thing to do is to wade into the water and save the child. Is it necessary to feel empathy for the child to commit this good act? Bloom argues not—"You don't need empathy to realize that it's wrong to let a child drown."[1] How we make moral decisions cannot be boiled down to empathy alone. In fact, if you tried to make most decisions based only on empathy, you'd be little more than a people-pleaser—not a morally superior person, but one with a poor sense of integrity.

You wouldn't know this from the way that empathy is discussed in popular culture. Empathy and morality have a close relationship, with headlines decrying a lack of empathy as the culprit behind any number of terribly immoral acts, from murder to genocide. Meanwhile, on an interpersonal level, it's fashionable in the 2020s for people to label themselves as "empaths," or highly empathetic people, as a bright, glaring virtue signal, while condemning others as "narcissists."

In fact, we often deny our empathy to those who are deemed to be immoral. Research has repeatedly shown that levels of empathy (the kind of "empathy" that can be measured by brain scans and self-report measures) are affected by moral characteristics.[2] If we believe someone is a bad person, we are less likely to empathize with them. You are less inclined to try to understand the perspective of a man who's lost his high-flying corporate job because he embezzled funds, for example. You'd also be less popular if you *did* try. There's a social pressure to empathize, but only with the right people—no one wants to be caught empathizing with a pariah. Stigma catches like a virus.[3]

Since those who supposedly "lack empathy" are often assumed to be less morally good, this means that these people find themselves—funnily enough—receiving little empathy from others. This is, in itself, anathema to empathy. It's a snake eating its own tail: How can anyone take the moral high ground claiming to be empathetic when they're villainizing entire categories of people for not experiencing, or expressing, this particular emotional process?

What it even means to "lack empathy" is not clear. People who describe themselves as lacking in empathy may, due to the slippery definition of empathy, all mean slightly different things by it. Some may mean that they struggle to imagine the experiences of others. Others might mean that they are not primarily motivated by the feelings of others, but rather by logic. Others still might mean that they're not very emotional people in general—their inner landscape a calm, still sea untroubled by the stormy winds and crashing waves felt by other people. As we've seen in the previous chapter, it could mean that someone's bodily trauma responses get in the way of their ability to connect to others, making it difficult for them to read and respond to the signals of other people. In each and every case, empathy is amoral. A person's declaration that they do not feel or experience it does not determine whether they are a good person, any more than it would if a person declared themself unable to feel anger, joy, or shame.

To truly see one another and forge real connections, we have to let go of binary "us versus them," "good and bad" narratives that divide us. This includes letting go of the idea that empathy itself is a moral virtue, and that only those who have this moral virtue deserve our empathy. Empathy is not a personality trait. It is not the litmus test of a good person. It is a skill we should strive to build not because it makes us morally superior, but because it is the thread in the fabric of human connection. Without it, we are alone. Empathy stitches us together.

In this chapter, we'll explore how it might actually feel to "lack empathy" and why this does not necessarily make someone immoral or predisposed to cruelty. We'll explore our societal obsession with "diagnosing evil," including through popular discourse about "empaths" and "narcissists," as a mythical way of identifying (and protecting ourselves from) the cruelty of others. Moving beyond these dehumanizing narratives, we'll briefly consider some alternative ways of making sense of violence and cruelty, before finally considering the difficult question of how we can extend empathy even to those whose actions we condemn or can't comprehend.

In order to practice empathy, even when it is uncomfortable, we must resist the desire to cast aside sections of society, to refuse their full personhood. To build a more inclusive, and dare I say, empathetic society is to accept everyone in their imperfections and their differences, and to hold others accountable for their actions rather than write them off as broken. Empathy sees the human in us all.

Helping without empathy

During my training to become a psychotherapist, I met a fellow trainee named Jackie. Though not yet formally diagnosed, Jackie has two autistic children, and is pretty sure that she's on the spectrum, too. I relate to her deeply, even though in many ways, Jackie and I couldn't be a more perfect case study of how wildly different autistic people can be. She is an extrovert who self-describes as an "over-sharer," while I am quieter, finding it difficult to speak in groups of people. She is a visual thinker who struggles to process written information; I'm a devout reader who finds it harder to process speech and presentations. And there's another crucial way we differ: Jackie tells me that she believes that she has low levels of empathy, and that this is related to her autistic traits.

On one blazing hot July day, I spoke to her about this, sitting in shaded deck chairs on the grounds of the university where we were both students. Jackie, who speaks in an effervescent, nonlinear way, leapt from topic to topic, occasionally pausing to point out a beautiful ginger cat stretching in the nearby sun.

Jackie said that she sometimes finds it hard to really imagine other people's points of view. "But I can see [their situation] from my own point of view," she said. She can imagine how she might feel in their shoes, even if their shoes don't quite fit. The closer their experiences are, the more able she is to do this. "If the same thing has happened to me, I can connect with you in that way. Or if I know somebody else who has gone through the same thing, I see how it has made them feel."

Jackie's description of her relationship to empathy chimes with the classic characterization of autistic people as lacking in cognitive empathy, the ability to imagine the minds of others. I told her that the more I've reflected on the pure, platonic ideal of empathy as the ability to "read the minds" of others, the more I believe that this isn't possible for any of us—and that people like Jackie are only more honest about it than most. But Jackie insisted that she is a "low empathy" person, and who am I to tell her otherwise? To try to talk her out of her own insights, I felt, would make me little better than the other institutions that systemically gaslight autistic people about their experiences. I draw on person-centered ideas in my therapy practice, which means that I accept every person's expertise on their own life. I try to meet Jackie's explanation of how her mind works without judgment.

When I pressed Jackie on what she feels that stops her from connecting empathetically to others, it surprised me how strongly I related to her answers. First of all, she highlighted the difficulty of being present in her own body. "I have to be comfortable in my environment before I can be present in the room," she explained. In the therapy room, "I have to make sure there's no ticking clock; that I'm comfortable in my clothes, in my surroundings. It might be noisy, too cold, too hot . . . you have to center yourself first, before you can be in the room for anybody else." Her insights resound with the recent advances in sensory neuroscience that we explored in chapter 3, which show how our sensory perception can relate to our expression of empathy and relationships with others.

And, just as we saw in chapter 3, it's not only the external world that can impact our empathy, but also how we experience our internal, emotional worlds. Jackie suggested her difficulties in being present—and therefore in empathizing with others—are related to her tendency to dissociate from her own feelings. "I can be flat; I'll talk about my trauma like it's a shopping list. And then something—a song, or a photo—will bring the emotion back, and I'll smell, taste, *feel* exactly what was going on. But I don't think about it until that happens."

For Jackie then, empathy is something that doesn't come naturally. It takes a forceful effort of will to bring herself into the room, and to try to imagine someone else's experience; she finds it hard to understand others at times, and finds herself overwhelmed by her own needs. For many, her account of what it's like to lack empathy might invite the question: If Jackie finds it so difficult to relate to others, why would she want to train to be a counselor? How can she help people without—by her own assessment—experiencing empathy?

Jackie might describe herself as having low empathy, but I have experienced her as someone with no shortage of compassion. She's a kind, warm person who fiercely advocates for what is right. Once, during a break from classes, she found me holding back sobs in the courtyard, and led me subtly away from the other trainees to ask what was wrong. I explained that I had been left frustrated by myself in the previous class, as I'd failed to verbally contribute anything. Despite my mind racing with thoughts, every word had died somewhere between my throat and my tongue. I was left feeling exhausted and unseen. Jackie soothed me by telling me that her son, who has similar autistic traits to mine, often experienced the same thing at school. She reassured me, walking laps around the university campus as the tears dried on my cheeks. Sharing stories about ourselves is not typically a way that we are taught to practice empathy—it could distract from the person you're empathizing with, instead centering the interaction on yourself—but in that moment, it was exactly the balm that I needed. I felt that no one understood me better than Jackie did.

There's also something to be said for the calming effect of being with a detached person who is *not* exactly mirroring your feelings. Jackie, before training to be a counselor, spent several years working as an emergency call receiver. She describes herself as someone who is calm in a crisis. She has spoken with people, many times, who were in the process of dying; she has sung to them, and kept them smiling, in their final moments.

Once, Jackie told me, she helped a woman trapped upside down in a car after a road traffic accident. She believes that her ability to distance herself from people in their most traumatic moments makes her more helpful to them. "If it's somebody else's life, I can deal with it," said Jackie. "I can separate myself from it." If there's a distressing story on TV and Jackie is unaffected whereas others are upset, this might read as coldness. But for the woman in the car, Jackie was able to stay calm and be helpful, because she held on to the simple fact: "It's not my life, it's her life."

Jackie's ability to disconnect from her own emotions might, at times, prevent her from wholly understanding how others feel—but it doesn't stop her, and in fact might even help her, to be a soothing presence for people when they need her the most. She is open, able to be vulnerable, and effusively kind. She is willing to work hard to understand other people. She doesn't always instinctively know how to help others, but she has dedicated her life to trying to do so.

Her experience flies in the face of the moralizing language that usually surrounds empathy. Being deficient in it makes you, by many accounts, a monster. The implication when someone is described as lacking in empathy is, at best, that they are unkind. At worst, it's that they're morally bankrupt, and possibly evil. Understandably, when being empathetic is understood to be a morally good personality trait, people want to identify with it. Some go as far as to call themselves "empaths."

Empaths and narcissists

The definition of an "empath" is, like the definition of empathy itself, diffuse. One online listicle titled "15 Signs You Might Be an Empath" lists the first sign, redundantly, as "You have a lot of empathy."[4] The term has been widely used in science fiction, and in parapsychology, the study of psychic phenomena, as in the work of psychiatrist and clairvoyant Dr. Judith Orloff. On her website, Orloff describes empaths as highly sensitive people who feel very intensely, or as she puts it, "angst-sucking sponges." The traits she associates with empaths include being labeled as "too emotional," feeling drained in crowds of people, and overeating to cope with stress.[5]

The term has gained a tribal popularity on social media.

On TikTok, there are millions of videos from "empath" influencers. One video with over two million views describes empaths as "very sensitive" people, in relation to both emotions and senses like sight and hearing. (It's interesting to note this overlap between the traits of an "empath" and the traits of an autistic person, or a person with sensory processing differences. In a 2024 study by Sheffield Hallam University, 78 percent of autistic respondents said they experience "hyper-empathy" so strongly that it causes them distress.[6]) The influencer, filmed in black and white and speaking over a mournful piano soundtrack, goes on to explain that empaths feel the feelings of others very deeply, get angry about violence and hate speech, and love animals "beyond anything."[7] A similar video from a therapist describes empaths as people who cry during sad scenes in movies, love to host parties, and self-sacrifice to help others.[8]

If we put aside the outlandish claims about empathy necessitating a desire to host dinner parties or adopt cats, what these descriptions tend to have in common is an emphasis on the porous nature of the empath. The difference between being empathetic and being an "empath" seems to lie in how easily overwhelmed empaths are by their emotional experiences. "We [empaths] feel everything, often to an extreme," writes Orloff in her book *The Empath's Survival Guide*, "and have little guard up between others and ourselves."[9] Rather than a "high level of empathy," this might be attributed to sensitivity and weak boundaries. To experience emotions intensely is not the same thing as being attuned to the emotions of others, though we often talk about these two phenomena interchangeably. As we've explored so far in this book, empathy is a conscious process between people seeking to understand one another and connect. When you're knocked out by a tidal wave of emotions, you may be less likely to meaningfully connect with others, and not necessarily be more empathetic.

On the other end of the empathy spectrum in today's popular discourse are narcissists. It's not uncommon for me to hear from clients in counseling sessions that they believe that people who have hurt them are narcissists—a popular buzzword denoting cold, calculated, self-centered people who "lack empathy." I say this with compassion, as someone who has, in the past, also armchair-diagnosed my own nemeses as narcissists, and understood my own trauma through a lens of what is called "narcissistic abuse." I, too, have lurked among one million others on the subreddit r/RaisedByNarcissists, where members congregate to discuss the experience of being raised by emotionally abusive or neglectful parents, or otherwise impacted by manipulative relatives and partners.

But in recent years, I've begun to notice that, while it's common to see people diagnose others as narcissists, it is much less common to hear from people diagnosed with narcissistic personality disorder (NPD). It's easy to understand why, given the stigma of the label "narcissist," and the inherent problems of self-awareness that are attributed to those with this diagnosis (if you think you are one, the logic goes, you're probably not). Compared to the vast following of r/RaisedByNarcissists, the subreddit r/NPD is host to only fifty-two thousand members. In a 2016 essay for *The New Yorker* titled "What Happens When We Decide Everyone Else Is a Narcissist," writer Jia Tolentino noted that our perception of who exactly falls into the category is subjective: "Millennials seem narcissistic to baby-boomer social scientists; men and women looking for love seem narcissistic to each other; analysis-resistant patients seemed narcissistic to Freud."[10]

In recent years, the "narcissist" has been joined by the intriguing figure of the "dark empath." This phrase arises from a 2021 psychological study that argues that while the so-called "dark triad" of personality types—Machiavellianism, narcissism, and psychopathy—have historically been associated with a lack of empathy, it may be possible for a person with such "dark" traits to also have a capacity for empathy. The researchers describe "dark empaths" as "a subpopulation who demonstrate a cluster of dark personality traits (psychopathy, narcissism, and Machiavellianism) combined with elevated levels of empathy."[11] The term caught on like the familiar verbal wildfire of the 2020s. It rapidly traveled from academia to social media to mainstream publications, with *The Guardian* describing a dark empath as someone "who appears to be caring and sensitive, but who is actually using those skills to further their own agenda,"[12] and *Vogue* calling them a "low-key saboteur."[13] It's now firmly part of our cultural lexicon. While I was writing this chapter, I received a gossipy text from a friend about an acquaintance who recently went on a handful of dates with a minor celebrity and described said celebrity as—my friend put this part in all-caps, accompanied by the skull emoji—a "DARK EMPATH."

There is some welcome nuance here, as the researchers behind the term "dark empath" separate the ability to feel or express empathy from the capacity to carry out morally bad acts. You don't have to be impaired in empathy, in other words, to be a bit of a prick. It isn't essential to understand someone else's point of view and feel their feelings to make good moral decisions; nor does it follow that if you cannot empathize with other people, you will therefore make morally bad decisions, or want to hurt them. Many people empathize with others and yet choose to hurt them anyway. Many people struggle to relate to others and yet choose to be kind.

Still, the idea of the "dark empath" is, at the end of the day, just another pejorative label that can be used to write people off. By trying to identify who might be a "dark empath," we exercise an "us versus them" mentality, believing that there is a monstrous subcategory of human that we can protect ourselves from, if only we learn how to spot them. This is something humans have done throughout history, and it did not begin with empath-narcissist discourse online. These othering narratives might comfort us—by creating the illusion that we can make sense of the inexplicable—but they do so at a cost: demonizing whole sections of humanity.

The pop-cultural fascination with labeling "dark empaths" and "narcissists" springs from a culture of psychiatric diagnosis. Many opponents of such language argue that it isn't appropriate for Redditors and TikTokers to dole out casual diagnoses of something as serious as NPD without the necessary psychiatric expertise. Taking this critique a step further, we might cast a skeptical eye over the history of psychiatric diagnosis itself. After all, unlike many other kinds of medical diagnostic processes, where blood or tissue samples give definitive test results, psychiatric diagnoses are more subjective. There is no gold standard diagnostic test for conditions like autism, schizophrenia, or borderline personality disorder—whether you have them depends on the opinion of the psychiatrist who observes and interprets your behavior in order to diagnose you. Psychiatrists may disagree with one another; you may disagree with them. These are liquid categories, existing in flux.

Diagnostic categories regularly shift along with what we consider to be "normal" or acceptable in society. The idea of the mentally "healthy" and/or neurotypical person is a social invention, and the ways in which people can deviate from that norm have changed over the decades. It was only a little over fifty years ago, in 1973, when the American Psychiatric Association voted to no longer classify homosexuality as a "mental disorder" in the DSM (*The Diagnostic and Statistical Manual of Mental Disorders*). Gender dysphoria is still medicalized today, with transgender and non-binary people required to obtain diagnoses and approval from clinicians to be able to access gender-affirming care.

It is in this context that the DSM enshrines which disorders, such as NPD, entail a "lack of empathy." But what we consider to be a "normal" amount or expression of empathy shifts according to society's norms. The idea that we can "diagnose" evil by medically identifying a lack of empathy is an attractive but illusory one. Attractive, because it protects us from the difficult work of asking what it is about ourselves and the world we've built that might create or be complicit in evil. Illusory, because as we've already seen, there is no empathy device in human brains that can be objectively identified, nor shown to be impaired. Still, time and again, we see our culture's thirst to pathologically label those who have committed violent crimes.

Diagnosing evil

In the 2000s and 2010s, autism was generally characterized as a disorder that caused people to "lack empathy," and could therefore lead people to commit acts of cruelty—hence the pervasive myth of the "autistic shooter." In recent years, the baton of this stereotype has been more or less passed to those diagnosed with personality disorders. In his 2011 book *The Science of Evil*, Simon Baron-Cohen argues extensively that a lack of empathy is the root cause of evil in humanity, but that autistic people "despite their difficulties with cognitive empathy are often caring individuals."[14] Meanwhile, those with personality disorders are not so redeemable. Psychopathy, narcissism, and BPD are, in his opinion, "unequivocally bad for the sufferer and those around them."[15]

The "autistic shooter" archetype largely emerged from the media, with frenzied reporting on autism diagnoses attached to mass shooters. Perhaps the most famous example is Adam Lanza, who carried out the Sandy Hook massacre of 2012, in which he killed twenty elementary school children and six adults. Lanza was autistic, a fact that was quickly publicized in the wake of the shooting. Reporting on Sandy Hook led to a 130 percent spike in calls to the Autism Speaks helpline in the days after the murders.[16] Former classmates of Lanza's spoke to the press about his autistic traits—such as being shy, awkward, and failing to make eye contact—as though they were missed clues that could have indicated that he would commit a violent crime.[17]

This kind of reporting encourages viewers to police one another, observing others through a lens of suspicion, the impact of which is usually felt most acutely by the most vulnerable members of our society. The autism advocate Morénike Giwa Onaiwu wrote about the effects of the wave of autism panic after Sandy Hook in a 2013 blog titled "Don't let them be autistic...," in which she details the fear she feels each time a horrific event is reported in the news. Onaiwu writes that she prays the perpetrator is not Black because "no matter how many of us are honest, law-abiding, kind, non-violent people, we are erased every time the person who has done something wrong has skin that looks like mine." Following the diagnosis of her children and herself as autistic, Onaiwu also began to pray that the killer was not autistic, as she noticed the reductive reporting linking autistic traits to violence. "Our differences should not be pathologized," she writes. "Our uniqueness should not be misconstrued as a threat. Our diagnosis should not be vilified in the way that it is ALL. THE. TIME."[18] Her blog condemns the way in which Black autistic people, already marginalized by racism, are pushed further to society's margins by the "autistic shooter" stereotype.

Over time, following a strong backlash from the autistic community and families of autistic people, the scapegoating narrative in the media began to shift. In a 2014 *New Yorker* profile, Adam's father Peter Lanza shuns the idea that autism might have played a role in his son's horrific actions, saying, "Asperger's makes people unusual, but it doesn't make people like this." He wonders aloud if another, missed diagnosis—possibly schizophrenia—might have been to blame instead. Quoting Baron-Cohen's book on evil, the reporter of the article notes that autistic people have a "lack of empathy," but only "cognitive empathy," and that Adam Lanza's actions may indicate that he was also a psychopath.[19]

In recent years, as autism awareness has continued to grow and diagnosis rates have shot up,[20] this has become the new narrative du jour linking a "lack of empathy" with violent crimes. Rather than autism, the culprit is another, more stigmatized psychiatric disorder. This was the case with reporting on Jonty Bravery, a seventeen-year-old who threw a young child from the tenth-story viewing platform of the Tate Modern gallery in London in 2019. The boy survived the fall, but incurred traumatic, life-changing injuries. Bravery, who is currently serving a minimum fifteen-year prison sentence, was diagnosed as autistic at the age of five.[21] In reporting on Bravery's crime, outlets including BBC News, the *Daily Mail*, Sky News, and the *Evening Standard* all referred to Bravery using the epithet "autistic teenager."[22] A 2021 article from *The Guardian* began, "An autistic teenager who threw a six-year-old boy from the Tate Modern...."[23] In 2023, this was amended to remove the word "autistic." A note at the bottom of the webpage declared that this action was taken "to more closely follow our reporting guidelines relating to autism."[24] After the Tate Modern attack, however, Bravery was also diagnosed with an antisocial personality disorder.[25] A serious case review blamed Bravery's actions on the lack of earlier recognition of his personality disorder, noting that professionals supporting him had failed to distinguish his "callous" traits from his autistic traits.[26]

The implication is clear: Autism is not to blame, but there is still a psychiatric explanation for what makes someone do evil things. The teenage murderer Scarlett Jenkinson, one of two young people convicted of killing British teenager Brianna Ghey in 2023, was noted to have autistic traits following her arrest, then similarly diagnosed after her conviction with "a severe form of conduct-dissocial disorder, one of the features of which is having no empathy."[27] In the wake of Lucy Letby's conviction for the murder of seven babies in 2023, the British press questioned openly whether she might be a psychopath, seeking a diagnostic label to make sense of the deaths.[28] These cases all show that our press and our criminal justice systems still rely on a psychiatric framework to make narrative sense of horrific crimes.

To understand a little more about what it's like to have one of the most stigmatized diagnoses, I spoke with M. E. Thomas, a lawyer, musician, and content creator who is well known for writing the 2013 memoir *Confessions of a Sociopath*. Thomas has an antisocial personality disorder, and self-describes interchangeably as both a sociopath and a psychopath,[29] two labels that are associated with a lack of empathy. Thomas wrote her book about being a sociopath under a pseudonym, but was quickly identified and "outed" in her real life. As a result, she tells me that she lost work, friends, and a sense of safety. She says that she was punished preemptively, not for anything she had done, but for the idea that she was capable of doing terrible things due to her diagnostic label. She alleges that one school where she was supposed to teach subsequently banned her from coming within a thousand yards of the campus.

"It obviously feels unfair," Thomas sighs on a video call, recounting the lawsuits she has brought against former employers for discrimination. Thomas often thinks about a conversation she once had with a mental health nurse who works with prisoners with antisocial personality disorders. The nurse told Thomas that she regularly observes other nurses in her place of work behaving coldly toward such patients, and generally treating them with mistrust. To Thomas, it seems that people in general are afraid of being tricked by those with personality disorders. Common sense dictates that they must not be kind to such people, or show them any empathy, because this could lead to being abused or exploited in some way.

Thomas has found that people are particularly guarded and mistrustful of her since she started sharing her diagnosis more openly. She describes the reactions of some colleagues who reran conversations they'd had in the past and exclaimed, "Maybe you were manipulating me the whole time!" Thomas rolls her eyes, adding with a flourish of dark humor, "Don't flatter yourself! Why would *you* be the target of my manipulation?"

Thomas's description of the mental health nurse and the suspicious colleagues rings true to me. I have seen fellow therapists and supervisors discuss personality disorders with a guarded, defensive air. Some of the things I have heard other therapists say about those with personality disorders have been pathologizing, and plain unkind. Many therapists write off those with personality disorders as being beyond their help, and even label those who seem to be failing to make progress in therapy as having a personality disorder.[30] It comes as little surprise to me that, when faced with such coldness from the very people who are supposed to support and care for them, those with the most stigmatized mental health labels would only internalize the idea that they themself are somehow broken, wrong, or evil. The "lack of empathy" label becomes a self-fulfilling prophecy.

Diagnosis can be an important explanatory tool. To many people—including me—their psychiatric diagnosis is a lifeline, a key to a community, a way of tuning into themself and their needs. As the disability theorist and writer Eli Clare has written, "Diagnosis wields immense power. . . . It opens doors and slams them shut."[31] While diagnoses can be a step toward healing, they can also lead to stereotyping—an aforementioned door slammed in the face of empathy. No person can be wholly explained by a label.

Stigmatizing diagnostic labels can end up functioning in a similar way to the criminal justice system, not only withholding empathy from the most marginalized people, but practically oppressing and disempowering them. By categorizing people into "good" and "bad," as Angela Davis would say, we "disappear" the people that we consider to be bad.[32] Both systems disproportionately target Black people, Indigenous people, and people of color. To give one example, Black people are diagnosed with schizophrenia at substantially higher rates than white individuals in both the US and the UK.[33] There is also a substantial overlap between those who are imprisoned and those who are diagnosed with some of the most stigmatized labels: In the UK, those in prison have been found to have at least double the likelihood of being diagnosed with a mental disorder, with 4 percent having a psychotic illness.[34] Criminalization and diagnosis are overlapping systems of control, and both are used to disproportionately oppress those who exist on society's margins.

When it comes to those who go on to commit violent crimes—those who abuse or hurt others—it may give us some temporary relief to imagine that if we had simply spotted their traits and correctly diagnosed them earlier with a "lack of empathy," we might have somehow been able to prevent their actions. This kind of magical thinking assumes that a person's diagnosis can fully explain their actions; that something as horrifyingly incomprehensible as violence could have been prevented by one intervention. At the root of this magical thinking is a desire to find out which category of people are the *bad ones*. There is a desire to know—scientifically, medically, empirically—who the "evil" people are in order to avoid, ostracize, and withhold our empathy from them.

But the biggest challenge to our empathizing abilities comes when we're confronted with those who we don't understand. Thomas, who believes that she does not experience what she calls emotional empathy (also known as affective empathy), tells me that she tends to get along very well with fellow "unempathetic" people, as they find it easy to understand one another. Interestingly, she finds it similarly easy to get along with those who report having high levels of empathy, because she finds those people are the ones most willing to put the time and effort into connecting with her.

"The people in the middle ground are not willing to extend that empathy, to consider things from other points of view," she says. To Thomas, most day-to-day displays of what would typically be called "empathy" are really performances engineered to make the empathizer look like a good person. "I hate to say it, but I think normal people are self-involved. They seem more concerned with how they are viewed by other people than anything else. People have a really hard time getting past that, and I think that's a really sad existence."

What would it look like to stop performing empathy for the purpose of seeming "good," and to really, truly empathize? A crucial part of it would be letting go of the idea that we can divide up humanity into "good" and "bad" people at all. Instead, we might sit with the discomfort that all of us contain both goodness and badness. We can judge people for actions that we condemn, while maintaining the view that no one is inherently, irredeemably bad.

There are no evil people

As a psychotherapist, it's part of my role to have some compassionate curiosity about why people do the things that they do. This desire to peek under the hood of humanity—or as I like to think of it, my professional nosiness—leads me to believe that there is more to people's worst impulses than a "lack of empathy" determined by a fault in their engine. The "autistic shooter" stereotype, the binary discourse around "empaths" and "narcissists," and the demonization of personality disorders all feed an age-old narrative that there are certain people who are "sick" and disrupt the peace of an otherwise well-functioning society. But to me, and to other psychotherapists who work in a non-pathologizing way, "evil" is not something biologically encoded in any of us, but rather, like many other things about being human, a product of our biology in combination with our relationships, society, and culture. I believe that immoral acts may emerge from deep wounds of trauma, in the broader context of societal power dynamics, and the failures of our systems to adequately protect and nurture vulnerable people.

When people are asked what they would do if they could time travel, many reply that their first act would be to kill the infant Adolf Hitler, long before he had a chance to rise to power in Germany. Some argue that this would not change the overall course of history—that if Hitler had not been the one to spearhead Nazi Germany, someone else would have done so. Philosophical pub debates like this ask us to consider whether cruelty is really something that can be located in an individual's psychology (as we suppose it is when we declare it a "lack of empathy"). Is looking at one person's psyche enough to explain why bad things happen?

I'd argue that it's not. I find myself thinking of the 2023 film *The Zone of Interest*, which documents the mundane domestic life of the Auschwitz commander Rudolf Höss and his wife, Hedwig. Though it focuses on a man who commits unthinkable atrocities, the film's central question is not how individuals become sick enough to carry out such acts, but how our society is built to normalize and contain such acts. It shows the sickening dissonance of soaking yourself in a paddling pool, or cultivating a row of green beans, while people scream in raw terror on the other side of your garden fence. The film forces its viewers to consider their complicity, and the ways we, as a society, turn away from horror. I was forced to turn toward myself: A prolonged black screen at the film's opening provides a stark mirror to popcorn-full mouths.

For over a century, psychoanalysts and psychotherapists have debated the nature of evil, and whether it comes from the individual or from society. Freud saw evil as a manifestation of the uncontrolled "id": the part of your psyche that's driven, selfishly, by your primal needs. Jung similarly characterized evil as part of the "shadow" self—the dark underbelly of your unconscious mind—running rampant, without being adequately balanced by the conscious, rational part of your mind.

I've personally always found these psychoanalytical perspectives to be a fairly bleak take on what it means to be human. Psychoanalytical ideas about evil suggest that we all contain a rabid selfishness at our core, and that if we didn't make a conscious effort to keep this primal self in check, we would all be self-centered and cruel. I've always been more drawn to person-centered, humanist psychology, as expressed by Carl Rogers. Rogers saw people as fundamentally good: He believed that all humans, given the right environment and resources, have the potential to be their best selves. He argued that "evil" arises from society and culture, not from individuals.

Rogers was criticized in his lifetime for being naive and overly optimistic. If we believe that all people are fundamentally good, and it is society that makes them evil, this still doesn't account for or explain every act of unthinkable cruelty. In the early 1980s, Rogers had a public exchange of letters on this subject with another prominent humanist thinker, Rollo May.[35] May was an existentialist psychologist and psychotherapist. His views were also rooted in humanist philosophy, but he had a less rosy view of humanity than Rogers did. In fact, he argued to Rogers that it's necessary to see not only the good in every person, but the potential for good *and* evil in every person. May wrote that, to be "realistic," "we must include a view of the evil in our world and in ourselves."

Like many existentialists, May believed it necessary to accept life's bad with the good to live authentically. To illustrate his point, May remembered being ill with tuberculosis in his teens. Looking around him, he observed that fellow patients who were hopeful and made light of their situations frequently died, while "those of us who lived with it, accepted it, struggled against it, recovered."[36] May's argument was that evil exists in society and culture *because* it exists inherently in humans—not the other way around—and it is healthier for us all to accept that we have this capacity for a little cruelty. Accepting that we all contain this potential can also allow us to have more empathy for those who we see as immoral. As they say, "There but for the grace of God go I."

As we explored in chapter 3, there's been a surge of interest in tracing the effects of trauma—particularly early childhood trauma—in recent years, and this has included an exploration of trauma's impact on a person's capacity to do immoral things. Trauma-informed ways of working are all about focusing not on what's wrong with someone, but on what happened to them. This is a more empathetic approach to the question of what we do with "bad" people, or people who commit immoral acts. Rather than see someone as irredeemable or even subhuman, we can try to understand what led to their actions. As clinical psychologist Lucy Johnstone describes it, traumatic situations like abuse or torture can lead us to find inventive ways of coping, like dissociation (or losing focus) and hearing voices; cruelty to others can be another "symptom" or coping mechanism like these. The message of the trauma-informed approach, as she defines it, is: "You have survived very difficult circumstances in the best way you could at the time. These strategies are no longer needed or useful and, with the right kind of support, you can learn to leave them behind."[37]

A key tool of the trauma-informed movement in psychiatry is the Power Threat Meaning Framework (PTMF). The PTMF was developed as a direct alternative to the DSM—where one is a list of disorders and illnesses, the other catalogues the many responses people might have to (or meaning they might make of) their trauma. The PTMF looks at the context of a person's "abnormal" behavior in their environment and society, and at the story that this behavior might be telling. It also recognizes the inherent variability of "disorders" of the human mind, noting that while diagnoses might help us identify patterns in "seemingly unintelligible actions," said actions can also be understood as arising from a stew of life experiences, social context, and biology, and how each individual person makes their own meaning from these factors.[38] A practitioner working with the PTMF could see someone experiencing paranoid thoughts or hallucinations, for example, and instead of diagnosing them with "psychosis," would seek to understand what happened to them in the past, how it affected them, and how these thoughts might have developed as a survival tactic.

This approach is deeply empathetic, because it seeks to understand someone's point of view, rather than writing them off as a "disordered" category of person. It does not treat any person as "evil"—to empathize fully, it's important to recognize that there are no evil people. I do not mean to be glib when I write this. I have judged others, and I have struggled, like anyone, to find my foothold in empathizing. Looking for the good in others—or even just trying to sit with the ambiguity of "this person contains both good and bad," rather than reach for the concrete certainty of diagnostic and stereotypical labels—is heavy work. The lessons I've learned in the therapy room have helped me begin to strengthen this muscle.

Our common humanity

In therapy, we talk of having "unconditional positive regard" for our clients. This means offering our clients total acceptance, regardless of what they say or do. Alongside empathy, this is one of the core conditions that Carl Rogers suggested all therapists should offer the people they work with. No matter what, we strive to create a space where someone can feel cherished, whatever failings or flaws they may have.

During my training, as I prepared to begin working

with clients, I grappled with what felt like the completely unattainable saintliness of this concept. Unconditional positive regard means viewing everyone as worthy of love, and as a good person—or at least, a person who is capable of good. I wondered, how on earth could I be expected to show unconditional positive regard if I was pushed beyond the limits of my ethical principles, or my values? What if I truly thought someone was deserving of my judgment, because their actions were immoral? What would I do if confronted with someone abusive, someone racist, someone homophobic?

I think, if they were being honest with themselves, most therapists who work with Rogers's core conditions would admit that "unconditional positive regard" is a slippery concept. As I noted earlier, Rogers was criticized in his lifetime for his idealism. Every therapist, I'm sure, struggles with the "unconditional" part at times. We have our limits. But in beginning to actually work as a therapist, I found that I was less confronted by the question of how to *practice* unconditional positive regard than I had been when puzzling over it in theory.

The truth was that unconditionally accepting people was not always easy, but it was easier than I had thought it might be. When a person allows you to get up close to them, makes themselves vulnerable, and shares a little of their world with you, it is much harder to judge them than it is to judge abstract others in your head. This is a known truism about empathy: It is easier to empathize with someone when you know them. One 2019 study confirmed this, as researchers found that empathy is difficult mental work, and as a result, the average person actively, strongly avoids empathizing with strangers.[39] When someone is presented to you as a distant idea—a caricature, a statistic, an archetype—it is hard for most of us to imagine life from their point of view. But when someone is in front of you, so close that you can see the sweat beaded on their forehead or hear their foot tapping anxiously on the ground, you can't deny their humanity.

Early in my career as a counselor, I worked with a client who, after a few sessions, confessed to me that he had used a misogynistic slur against an ex-girlfriend during a fight with her. The memory of this moment of emotional violence was heavy as he set it down in the space between us, his downcast eyes trailing along the floor as he spoke. There was something like remorse in his voice, but it was heavily shielded by prickly defiance. A sense of: *I hadn't meant to—she made me do it.*

As my client shared his story with me, I felt I could hear another perspective behind his words, struggling to get through, like light through a curtain. The perspective of his ex. I had, at this point, worked with numerous women who had experienced emotional abuse like this client was describing. As a woman, I had also experienced the sharp, serrated edges of misogyny and abuse myself. It was hard to maintain my empathy for this client when the more easily imaginable, heartstring-pulling perspective of

Empathy is amoral

his ex was competing for my attention. With each deflection or justification of his actions, my client pushed me further away. The night after our session, I dreamt that he was towering over me, growing taller and taller until I was swallowed entirely by his shadow.

After talking it through with my supervisor and fellow counselors, and sitting with my feelings of discomfort for a few days, I realized a few things that helped me to work toward empathizing with this client again. First of all, showing him compassion did not mean that there was no need to challenge him or hold him accountable. Empathy is not all affirmations and validation. It can also be a process of offering what the activist and writer adrienne maree brown would call "loving corrections"—kind but honest feedback.[40] In this case, I decided to invite my client to think about how his ex might have felt, or even how he himself felt—genuinely, deep beneath the molten surface of his rage—after hurting someone else.

Secondly, I recognized that there was a frightened part of my client that felt he needed to put down others to survive. In keeping with my trauma-informed ethics, I explored with him: Where did this fear come from? Seeking to understand his actions was not the same thing as codoning them. It was doing the delicate work of unpacking the violence that had been stitched into his psyche and his nervous system—and this delicate work might support him to feel calmer, and therefore inflict less pain in the future. I saw myself as helping to safeguard the other people in this client's life, by empathizing with his rage and giving it an outlet. After all, being isolated, marginalized, and stigmatized drives people only deeper into rotten, radicalized echo chambers and sadistic mindsets. If someone leaves my counseling room with their fists slightly unclenched, insults fading on their tongue, I feel that my work has value.

I did not have to see my client as morally virtuous, nor in the right, nor did I even have to always like him, to offer him meaningful support in this way. I began to form my own interpretation of "unconditional positive regard": It's about seeing people as unconditionally human. It was through my work with this client, and others who challenged me, that I learned the most about accepting people as they are: in their complications, their contradictions, their messiness.

An alternative to the concept of "unconditional positive regard" is the idea of "common humanity." I first came across the term in a book about self-compassion by Dr. Kristin Neff,[41] inspired by Buddhist philosophy. Neff describes common humanity—the recognition of your own experiences as being shared by other people—as a vital component of showing kindness to yourself. It's all about moving your focus away from your individual self and toward the collective. Counterintuitively, making this mental shift may allow you to be kinder to yourself, as you accept that your feelings are not a distortion of your individual psyche, but a part of the colorful tapestry of being human. I'm not the only person who has ever felt the pain of heartbreak, for example. When my heart is broken, I can find solace in stepping into the vast ocean of experienced heartbreak documented by humans before me (for instance, I can listen to an Amy Winehouse album), reminding me that I am not alone. We can relate more strongly to one another, become closer to one another, and show more compassion to one another by recognizing the experiences that we share as human beings.

An important part of this is not othering people, even those who do hurtful or immoral things. In working with clients, for me this means trying not to look at people through a medical lens that explains their actions as symptoms of a disorder, and instead, trying to understand the emotions beneath their actions, the texture of the world from their point of view.

Of course, I have the emotional reserves to do this as a therapist because I am not personally impacted by what my clients do outside of the therapy room. If you've been hurt by someone, it would understandably be much harder to empathize with them—and there is no obligation for you to do so. No victims of abuse should be compelled to show compassion or forgiveness to their abuser; no oppressed person owes kindness to their oppressor. But something we can all do is avoid dehumanizing others in our language. Dehumanization is the biggest barrier to empathy there is.

What this might look like, day to day, is stopping before

calling someone a "dark empath," and instead articulating the exact harm that person has caused, and asking them to be accountable for it. I say this as someone who has themself in the past happily decried an ex for being a "narcissist," or a landlord for being "sociopathic." These days, I try to use language that is more specific. For example, I might say that my ex treated me unkindly, or that my landlord is a capitalist wealth hoarder. I'm kidding—mostly—but I do genuinely try my best to avoid pathologizing or generalizing. This is not always easy. When speaking from pain, we reach instinctively for labels like weapons, in a combination of self-protection and righteous anger. That's part of my point: None of us is perfect. Moral perfectionism is an enemy of empathy—we should hold others accountable for their actions, but if we expect them to be morally perfect in order to receive our empathy, then we are not forming authentic connections. We are living in a fantasy.

Empathy is not a trait that you either have or don't have, therefore making you a good or bad person. It is also not something that should be reserved only for morally good people. Practicing it is not about being a more virtuous individual; it is a vital building block of a better world for us as a collective. I see it as something more like exercise. Exercise is something we can all do, though being active might look different for every person, depending on all kinds of biological, social, and cultural factors. Still, whether you're competing in the Olympics or doing some gentle stretches, it's broadly agreed that moving our bodies is something we can all have a go at, and we can all benefit from. It's a healthier way to live. Our ability to relate to and connect with one another is, similarly, a skill we can all cultivate and grow richer from. There is liberation in finding our common humanity. Plus, like stretching your aching back in the morning or hitting your stride during the second mile of a sun-streaked run, it feels good. It gets your heart beating, and reminds you that you're human.

5

Empathy is radical

What many people think is empathy can land more like pity. My friend Steven, who is deafblind, finds this to be particularly true in his day-to-day life. "I've lost track of the number of times a taxi driver has said to me, 'I don't know how you do what you do, mate,'" he tells me. "I know they see it as a compliment. They genuinely think they're praising me. But it's like ... what do you *expect* me to do?"

Steven laughs, and sighs, as the unspoken answer to his question hangs in the air between us. When taxi drivers tell him they don't know how he does it—when he's just going about his day, trying to get to work in the back of their cab—they're imparting a genuine bafflement at the question of what it must be like to be him. They may even be suggesting that to them, Steven's everyday life seems so difficult as to be barely worth living. No matter how well-intentioned, suggesting that Steven's life must be unimaginably difficult is alienating for him.

Often, those with social power make do with offering sympathy to those more marginalized than themselves. Those who have social power are usually those in the majority, or part of a dominant class, which could mean white people, able-bodied people, cisgender people (those who identify with the gender they were assigned at birth), wealthy people, and so on. From a position of power, pity is much more comfortable than empathy, because it doesn't challenge the status quo. This is a crucial difference between empathy and being "nice." Niceness may make the person giving it feel good about themselves more than it actually improves anything for the person receiving it. By feeling sorry for someone in a more marginalized position than your own, you only solidify the preexisting power dynamic between you. Empathy is much more radical. To truly practice it, you need to redistribute a little of your power.

In this chapter, we'll uncover what this radical empathy might look like. We'll consider the lessons of the "double empathy problem," the theory that teaches that empathy is a two-way process of communicating—and we'll also consider the theory's limits, and its applications beyond the autistic community. We all find it easier to relate to others in our cultural in-groups, and people of any marginalized group might find themselves receiving less empathy from the majority.

How do we work to overcome these structural barriers to empathy and build connections with people who are different from ourselves? It begins with recognizing how power and oppression shape the society we live in, and how those power dynamics exist inside you. To learn more about this, we'll look at some of the principles of anti-oppressive counseling: therapy that acknowledges and challenges systemic oppression. Finally, we'll consider what an anti-oppressive approach to empathy might look like in day-to-day life.

Empathy is sometimes discussed as though it were a kind of social nectar, sweetening and pacifying. We're told that it neutralizes social differences. But in reality, it's a skill in building authentic relationships, which means that it is often uncomfortable and far from sweet. To empathize, we must confront our differences head-on. The systems that are unconsciously embedded in us—systems of white supremacy, colorism, misogyny, heteronormativity, capitalism, and so on—will inevitably show up in our relationships with each other. So, empathy is political. How could it not be? Each of us contains a whole world—and each of us contains *the* world, sharp little pieces of its unjust systems lodged between our bones and organs like shrapnel.

Cultural shortcuts to empathy

I first met Steven while we both worked for a national disability charity. Steven is a tall man who carries his height gently, with a soft voice and kind smile. Though we worked together for a couple of years, we crossed paths in the office only occasionally, both of us working part-time, hybrid hours. Steven is deafblind, and has cochlear implants that enable him to communicate with others using speech. He is also—he discovered in his thirties—autistic. We began to develop a friendship over Microsoft Teams when we discovered this commonality, along with a mutual appreciation for the music of Taylor Swift.

Steven remembers that he always felt "different," and found it hard to build relationships when he was at school. Social isolation was a common theme in his childhood and teenage years, which he puts down to his difficulties with the "to-and-fro" of relationships. "I either feel like I'm too friendly, or too stand-offish," he reflects. "Things like small talk are really difficult." Thinking back on his school days, he references a dark joke he saw on X (formerly known as Twitter) about the uncanny ability of school bullies to "diagnose" autism. "It's awful, but it's true, isn't it?" He's not wrong: Autistic children have been shown to be at higher risk of bullying and victimization at school than their neurotypical peers.[1] One 2017 study showed that even among adults, non-autistic people tend to take an instant, knee-jerk dislike toward autistic people on first meeting.[2]

Empathy is radical

Steven hasn't found his autism diagnosis to be a "magic bullet" that's made his feelings of being an outsider go away, but it has given him some insight into his communication difficulties, and more importantly, some self-compassion. He now feels more able to accept that some social situations are tough for him, knows which accommodations are helpful for him, and has a way to explain to people why he's struggling. In general, he's found that being able to describe his experience to his coworkers using the language of autism has engendered more empathy for him in the workplace.

Steven's story is a relatable one to me, and a common one among late-diagnosed autistic people. Diagnosis can be a gift. Although the stigma of a psychiatric label can block empathy, the clarification of your needs can also be a kind of Rosetta Stone—allowing easier communication and understanding between ourselves and the neurotypical world. It is moreover the key to unlocking an easier, more automatic kind of empathy between us, fellow autistic people. I felt empathy from Steven when, following a four-hour cross-department meeting at the charity we both work for, he sent me a message to check if I was feeling overwhelmed. I was struck by his kindness in that moment, but even more so, his intuition. He knew that four hours under fluorescent lights, talking, listening, and masking in a large group of people was bound to be draining for me. He could implicitly understand how I was feeling—and I feared no judgment when I told him that I was indeed feeling overwhelmed.

With another colleague, I might have tiptoed gingerly around the truth, hesitant to admit that I was anything less than capable of the same amount of work as everyone else; fearing that the near-invisible nature of my overwhelm was too difficult for others to understand. But with Steven, I knew that if I was direct about how I was feeling, he would not question the reality of my experience, and would certainly not question whether I was capable or worthy of my job. I knew that he might even be asking because he was feeling the same way himself.

Steven and I found in each other a coworker with whom we could discuss autistic experiences like meltdowns or stimming with mutual, nonjudgmental ease. It can be a relief to find someone in life who speaks the same language that you do. Suddenly, in the midst of a lifetime filled with faltering, stuttering conversations, there's someone with whom the words flow.

But while Steven and I have been brought closer to one another by our baseline empathy for one another's experiences, there is also a great deal that separates us. It's not as simple as saying that both of us being autistic means that we automatically "get" one another; as with any other person in the world, I have some overlap with Steven's experiences, and some distinct differences. There are ways in which we can feel into each other's experiences easily, and ways in which we can't. For instance, I'm a woman, and Steven is not. Steven is deafblind, and I've no idea what it's like to navigate the world with those sensory differences, and to be read by other people as visibly disabled. And besides, even if we were the same gender, or had the same disabilities, there are likely to be other differences in our backgrounds, our cultures, or even our personalities that make it impossible for us to fully know what it's like to be in the shoes of the other.

Empathy is not something you do to another person, but that two people share together. The "double empathy problem" that we encountered in chapter 2 demonstrates this: Empathy is a two-way process of communicating, rather than a one-way process of emoting. If you have some baseline similarities with another person—for example, you're both autistic—then it's more likely that you'll understand one another more easily. Like Steven and I, you might experience some shortcuts to empathy: We can more easily grasp pieces of each other's internal worlds, because they are also pieces of our own.

I have experienced some of this ease of connection in autistic-only or autistic-led spaces since my diagnosis. In online meetings, I've felt an immense surge of relief from knowing that it was socially acceptable to sit with my camera turned off, or to type instead of talk, if I felt that I needed to that day. This acceptance was the key difference between these spaces and the more normative spaces I'd spent so much of my life inhabiting—other ways of being weren't demonized or excluded by default. I was not chastised for being too quiet, nor were others chastised for interrupting or talking at length. It was a blessing to not have negative intentions being prescribed to me for behaving the way I naturally wanted to. It was not assumed that I was cold, uncaring, or eschewing connection of any kind if my approach to connection looked a little different.

Spending time with fellow neurodivergent people can feel like the relief of getting home from the office and taking off painful shoes. The research supports this: In one qualitative study published in 2020, researchers interviewed autistic people to find out whether they felt more comfortable, and experienced more connection, with fellow autistic friends and family than neurotypicals. This investigation found that autistic people often felt a pressure to "mask" and conform with neurotypical expectations when around neurotypical friends and family members. Meanwhile, with fellow autistics, there was more flexibility around what was considered a "good" way to spend time together, with one participant commenting, "There is no pressure to talk. If there are silences it is not awkward because there is a shared understanding that silence is nice."[3]

Of course, it's too simplistic to expect that all autistic people, by virtue of being autistic, will get along with one another. Some of the groups I took part in reminded me of the heterogeneity of the spectrum, and how in fact, sometimes we autistic people can be the worst possible thing for one another. As someone who is very quiet and introverted, and sensitive to loud noises, for example, I can find it difficult to be around people who talk a lot and loudly, as some other autistic people do. Autistic people are as contradictory and conflict-ridden as any other cross-section of society, and any other marginalized group. We have intersectional identities and face intersectional oppressions.

It would obviously be reductive to claim that all gay people, for example, share similar personality traits and get along well with one another. Within the bracket of "gay," there are millions of unique perspectives and lived realities. The same is true for any other group of people. This is where there's room to expand the double empathy problem, considering the many different ways that our social and cultural identities can impact our ability to truly see each other.

The infinite empathy problem

As things stand, researchers studying the double empathy problem have largely looked at one axis of empathy—whether the participants are autistic—but it's clear that the theory has huge potential beyond this. In a 2022 article reflecting on ten years of the double empathy problem, the theory's creator, Damian Milton, wrote that the future of research in this area needs to look at how other intersectional oppressions also impact empathy.[4] While research has shown that the double empathy problem exists between autistic and non-autistic people, the narrow scope of this research to date has not accounted for differences *within* the autistic community—for example, between speaking and nonspeaking autistic people. It also doesn't account for the ways other intersecting identities—race, gender, class, sexuality, physical disabilities, and so on—can impact the ways in which we empathize with one another. Most crucially of all, there's room to take this theory beyond autism research and recognize how our identities influence our experiences of empathy, no matter who we are. The double empathy problem doesn't quite go far enough—what we're dealing with is more like an infinite empathy problem.

Since Milton first spoke about the double empathy problem, lots of studies have been carried out to prove that it exists. For example, one group of researchers in 2020 sorted seventy-two participants into nine groups: three autistic groups, three non-autistic groups, and three mixed groups. They found that information was transferred between people equally well—and rapport was good—in the all-autistic and all-non-autistic groups. It was in the mixed groups that problems arose.[5] Another study, carried out in 2021, played a series of videos representing both autistic and non-autistic people to an audience of neurotypical viewers. The viewers rated the non-autistic people they saw in the videos as more "likeable." They disliked the autistic people they saw due to their awkwardness, and among other traits, their perceived lack of ability to empathize.[6]

Results like these confirm Milton's suspicions that those with perceived "empathy deficits" are actually just communicating differently, and being judged differently by their peers—but we must be careful about generalizing too broadly from academic studies like these, which usually test a small, fairly unrepresentative sample of people. Of the autistic participants included in the 2020 research, all communicated verbally, didn't have learning disabilities, and were diagnosed as autistic in adulthood. This represents a specific, privileged cross-section of the autistic community: those like me, who might be referred to as "high-functioning,"* or as having low support needs.** We don't know that these people, if placed in a mixed group with autistic people with learning disabilities and higher support needs, would be any more effective at building rapport and communicating than non-autistic people would be.

As a minimally speaking person, Hari Srinivasan, the neuroscientist we first met in chapter 3, has experienced

---

* "High-functioning" is not a term I like to use myself, which is why I use it in scare quotes here. This is mainly because, to me, it feels dehumanizing. To be called "high-functioning" makes me feel like I'm being described as though I were a microwave or a motorbike. In online neurodiversity advocacy spaces, "functioning" labels are vehemently debated. There are plenty of anti-capitalist critiques of the labels, which I think make good sense—no person's value should be determined by how well they "function" in a labor market. There are also some people who self-identify with the "high-" or "low-functioning" label, and find that it usefully describes their experiences. I believe in each person's right to determine what language most accurately applies to their own life.

** Many prefer the language of "support needs" to "functioning"—it shifts the focus away from "how well can you function?" to "what support do you need?"

varying degrees of empathy from speaking autistic people and neurotypical people alike. "I've had some amazing neurotypical folks cross my path on my journey, who have really helped and supported me," he says. He also points me toward a comment he once read on an online forum that demonstrates an "utter lack of empathy and lack of compassion by autistics toward other autistics. The comment reads: "Surprisingly, 'severe' autism is not always the biggest obstacle to employment or even personal happiness. . . . Higher functioning individuals are sometimes at a greater disadvantage because they may be struggling to 'pass' for normal."

We can check off a recognizable list of attributes that illustrate a lack of empathy in this comment: It speaks on behalf of a group of people rather than allowing them to speak for themselves; it makes a sweeping generalization about them; and it diminishes their experience, pitting their suffering against that of another group. For Hari, reading it was like a gut punch. "I'm so disappointed in my own community at times for their insensitivity," he says. "You don't get to negate someone else's disability to prop up your own. Every group has its own sets of issues, and we should not be trampling on the requirements of others."

The double empathy problem is therefore not cut and dry. Some autistic people may have more effective communication with their neurotypical caregivers, who have taken the time to get to know them and understand them deeply, than with other autistic people. Some autistic people may find themselves feeling excluded from the "autism community" because it's a space that is not immune from the white supremacy, homophobia, transphobia, classism, and other systems of oppression found in the rest of society. Just like in any other group, whether it's the LGBTQ+ community or a faith community, having this one thing in common does not guarantee affinity and attunement between all members.

Racism is a prominent barrier to empathy for autistic people of color. Research by the National Autistic Society into the experiences of Black and minority ethnic autistic people found that in the UK, many face extra challenges in getting diagnosed, finding appropriate support, and communicating with professionals.[7] Anecdotally, it's not only accessing support via healthcare that presents challenges, but finding a place in an overwhelmingly white autistic community, too.

One person who has struggled with this sense of unbelonging is Tyla Grant, an autistic podcaster, writer, and creative strategist. "I spent so long not feeling like I fit in with the general population," Tyla tells me in her lilting Mancunian accent. "Now I have this whole community, who I'm told that I should be able to fit in with, and I'm like ... Nah. The vibes are massively off."

Tyla was diagnosed as autistic at seventeen, after a long period of being mislabeled with various other mental health diagnoses. She turned to online content creation while she was at university, building a following with her YouTube videos and using her platform to establish a mutual aid fund to help other Black neurodivergent people gain access to diagnoses. Now, in her spare time, she creates longform, thoughtful podcasts. Tyla hasn't found the "autism community" to be a place where she feels peaceful harmony. She has a discomfort with calling herself an autism advocate, or even with attending autism support groups or community spaces, she tells me, "because of some autistic people's lack of [empathy] to people who don't look like them and think like them." For Tyla, experiencing a lack of empathy from others is exhausting—and constant. It's not only in the "outside" neuronormative society, but everywhere, that she experiences racial biases combined with ableism as a Black autistic woman. "It's extra mental work to account for other people's lack of empathy," she sighs. "Actually, I wouldn't even say it's a lack of empathy—it's a lack of willingness to be empathetic. Because they can do it for other people. But it's when people are dealing with a group that's alien or other to them—it's locked away."

These intersectional differences in the autism community are differences of power. Those with closer proximity to whiteness, able-bodiedness, heteronormativity, and other socially dominant forces, tend to be safer. Autistic people of color, and those with more marginalized identities, face oppressions that more privileged autistic people in the community don't have to encounter. For a white person, a failure of empathy from a neurotypical person might mean rejection from a job application process or friendship. For a Black person, the same lack of empathy may be further intensified by racism, and lead to additional threats like the higher risk of state violence.

There are many examples of autistic people of color being brutalized by police. In 2025, the nonspeaking Latino teenager Victor Perez was killed by Idaho police after a neighbor dialed 911. He was just seventeen.[8] In 2024, another nonspeaking autistic boy, fifteen-year-old Ryan Gainer, was killed by police in California. Ryan's friends described him as having a "big, bright, welcoming, safe smile" and being the "sweetest soul."[9] Gainer was shot by police after they were called to his house as he was having a mental health crisis. Gainer joins a long list of Black autistic people killed by police, including the self-described "introvert" Elijah McClain, and Osaze Osagie, both of whom were killed in 2019.

In people of color, and Black people particularly, autistic traits that are read as "awkwardness" in white people may be read as threatening, or even criminal. The consequences of this are real and ever-present. They're powerfully brought to life by Minneapolis-based AuDHD Somali poet Said Shaiye in his poem "Black Muslim Autistic Man Walks Thru Airport.docx."* Shaiye writes:

---

* AuDHD is a portmanteau describing the experience of being autistic and having ADHD.

> Thinking about how hard it is to make eye contact with people on a good day, let alone when I'm having a nervous anxiety breakdown in an airport. Because I'm Black. Because I'm Muslim. Because I am an alleged terrorist. Because I can't make eye contact to save my life.[10]

While I might empathize with Shaiye's pain at making eye contact, as a white person, I can't claim to experience the same life-threatening fear that he does when a gaze goes unmet. Our autistic experiences are not the same. All of which is to say that though the "double empathy problem" has radically reframed how we think about empathy in an undeniably positive way, it does not quite go far enough. Whether autistic or not, we also need to consider all the other ways in which our identities inform who we empathize with, and who we don't. And, most importantly, we need to consider the power dynamics at play behind those identities. Because power and politics shape everything—even empathy.

The politics of empathy

Who we find ourselves empathizing with most easily is not just a question of similarities and differences—it is politically engineered. We are deliberately invited by the dominant culture to empathize with people in the social majority, and to turn away from those on the fringes. On mental health awareness days, for example, we listen to stories of people who overcame anxiety and depression. But those who struggle severely with more stigmatized mental health issues—those who may be experiencing homelessness, who struggle with substance abuse, or who otherwise challenge social norms of acceptability—are largely forgotten. Learning how to swim against the current of easy empathy, and instead really fighting to empathize when you feel uncomfortable, is crucial. We cannot truly empathize without recognizing how power shapes our world.

To be neutral, or to be oblivious to power dynamics at play, is to take the side of the oppressor, demonstrating a deep failure of empathy, which forces marginalized people only further into the margins. This was clear in the public reaction to an article published by Brené Brown in 2024. Brown's work on empathy, which I cited in chapter 1, is wildly popular. She has spread academic insights into empathy through teachings that are compassionate, clear, and accessible. In February 2024, Brown published an essay titled "Not Looking Away" on the genocide in Gaza, which she described as "the Israel-Hamas war." In the essay, Brown asserted her support for nonviolence, her wish for peace, and her love and support for both Jewish and Israeli, and Palestinian and Muslim people.[11] While this may sound innocuous on the surface, Brown received a swift and widespread outcry from many of her devoted followers. This was because the neutrality of her statement failed to acknowledge the extremely uneven reality of the genocide unfolding in Palestine, and the history of settler occupation and colonial violence from Israel. Brown later published a second essay titled "Listening + Learning," in which she apologized for misrepresenting the power asymmetry between Israel and Palestine, and set out her plan to examine her own biases.[12]

Brown is only one person among many public figures and media outlets who have misrepresented the Palestinian genocide in this way. I use her as an example here because her popular academic work has made her a public authority on empathy, and yet, ironically, her article deprived Palestinians of empathy by failing to accurately represent their reality. As the Palestinian American author and psychologist Hala Alyan asked, in an essay for *The New York Times*, "Why Must Palestinians Audition for Your Empathy?" The essay pierces through the surreality of a mainstream media depiction of an even-handed war, and asks why Palestinian civilians being brutally killed are not afforded empathy—an empathy that would require acknowledging the reality of their situation. "Palestinian slaughter is too often presented ahistorically, untethered to reality," she writes, drawing attention to the way the media criminalizes Palestinian people. "To earn compassion for their dead, Palestinians must first prove their innocence."[13] Alyan asks us to consider who our empathy reaches for most easily, to notice that discrepancy within ourselves, and to get uncomfortable about it.

Empathy is radical

On a person-to-person level, power imbalances poison our relationships in the form of bias. When someone with more social capital struggles to empathize with someone with less, they might fill in the gaps in their understanding with assumptions or stereotypes. For example, a native English-speaking person who struggles to connect with an immigrant who speaks English as a second language might be invited, by the media and culture that surrounds us, to interpret this struggle through the lens of racist and xenophobic ideas about immigrants. Meanwhile, the other person faces the immense pressure of earning their right to empathy by performing the role of the "good immigrant"—attempting the Herculean task of overcoming those stereotypes and assumptions.

This is why being aware of your own position in society, and how it shows up in your relationships, is a critical aspect of empathy. It would be naive to think that you see everyone equally clearly, no matter who you are. The world we live in clouds the lenses we look through. The more power you have over the person you're interacting with, the cloudier those lenses may be, and the more effort it may take to wipe them clean.

Social power also manifests in certain people being viewed as more "empathetic" than others by default. Just take a look at the field of therapy: The British Association of Counselling and Psychotherapy—the professional board of which I'm a member—reported in 2024 that over 90 percent of its members were white.[14] Meanwhile, the

Empathy Takes Action

UK Council for Psychotherapy reported in 2023 that almost three quarters of its members were women.[15] It's no surprise to anyone working in the field that white women are massively overrepresented in it, making it a very inviting field for people like me, and a hostile one for many others. Of course, this doesn't mean that white women are more empathetic than anyone else. It means that white women like me are socialized to recognize that our value is entwined with being "empathetic," and to express compassion for others in certain socially acceptable ways that become a stand-in for what is considered "empathy." If you ask me, real empathy is something more disruptive, and something much less polite.

As I trained to become a therapist, I found myself deeply frustrated with the profession's approach to "diversity and inclusion." The idea of working with people of other cultures and backgrounds to yourself was presented as though patched on to therapeutic work, rather than a fundamental thread that runs through it. The teaching also often assumed that the counselor would be someone who is part of the majority, while their prospective clients would be the people of color, the working-class people, the neurodivergent people, the queer or transgender people, the fat people, the Mad people.* Not only was this othering, but the teaching didn't go far enough. Without considering how society and

---

* I use the terms "fat" and "Mad" in the tradition of the fat liberation and Mad pride movements.

culture shape your relationship with the person in front of you, and actively working to dismantle power imbalances between you, your attempts at empathy are little more than platitudes. As much as we don't like to admit it, therapists hold power over our clients. If we're not conscious of that, and actively trying to redress that balance, we run the risk of replicating the systems that harm people. For example, a straight therapist might subtly communicate their own homophobic discomfort when working with a gay client opening up about chemsex, or a white therapist might re-traumatize a person of color by being defensive on the topic of race.

Acknowledging and working to dismantle systemic oppression in counseling is known as "anti-oppressive" practice. Originating in the field of social work, the idea of practicing empathy in an "anti-oppressive" way is about recognizing the ways in which our society oppresses people of certain identities and working hard to make sure that oppression is not reenacted or reinforced in the way that you care. It's knowing that people have differences, that these differences give us different amounts of power, and that it's our duty as people working in supportive roles to try to actively neutralize power imbalances between us and those we support.[16]

In practice, this might mean not using interventions like calling the police when a person of color is in distress, but instead drawing on community support by calling their emergency contacts. It could mean offering practical assistance to someone navigating a complicated process like claiming asylum or disability benefits. It might even be something as small as acknowledging your differences with someone, to show them that you're willing to talk about your identity nondefensively, and asking how best you can show up for them. To be anti-oppressive is to be proactive about addressing the ways oppression shows up in our interpersonal relationships. This idea is not only an important one for psychotherapists, but for all of us in learning how to better empathize with people who are in more marginalized positions in society than ourselves.

Some of the key principles of anti-oppressive counseling practice can, I believe, also inform a more equitable day-to-day practice of empathy. Four key components of anti-oppressive empathy that we can all learn from are: seeing the systems around the feelings, believing others, learning about worlds beyond our own, and surrendering power.

To learn more about anti-oppressive practice, I spoke to an expert on the subject. Myira Khan is a psychotherapist and clinical supervisor based in Leicester. Myira's book *Working Within Diversity* was critical for me during my training—when I was frustrated with the DEI offered elsewhere, I found she has practical exercises and strategies for working with people of different backgrounds and social identities in a truly empowering, non-othering way. In the opening pages of her book, Myira describes how she felt alienated, as the only Muslim woman on her counseling course, by "diversity and difference" training that primarily spoke to white counselors about how to empathize with clients of color. She never saw training materials that showed a Muslim woman sitting in the counselor's chair.

This discrepancy "assumes who has the capacity, availability, credibility, skills, knowledge to be the helper," Myira says to me. "And it makes huge assumptions of who needs to be 'helped,' and who is the 'helpee,' very often positioning minoritized identities as those in need of help." Framing counseling in this way sends an implicit message, as Myira points out, that only one type of person is predisposed to be empathetic. "It perfectly sets up the oppressive dynamic of the white savior." To move past white saviorism and toward real empathy, Myira says, begins with really interrogating and reflecting on society's hierarchy of power and your own position in it—and how that impacts the way you relate to others. More than just feeling for someone, you have to understand how their experience is shaped by their position in society. "For me, empathy is beyond a feeling. Empathy is about holding capacity and space for somebody's entire lived experience."

Central to this practice is what Myira calls "cultural empathy," which involves seeing the systems that surround someone's emotional experience. To illustrate the concept, she tells me to picture that I'm being handed a helium balloon. "Imagine that that balloon is a client saying to you, 'I feel sad,'" she continues. "You catch the balloon, and you give it back to the client—via a restatement, paraphrase, or reflection. That's empathy in the traditional sense.

"Cultural empathy would be the client giving you that balloon, and then you tie a ribbon and a balloon weight to it. You ground the feeling in a context. And that's what you give back to the client."

Cultural empathy is empathy plus weight. It not only acknowledges your feelings individually, but sees the systems around the feelings. This grounds your emotional experience in the cultural context that gives it meaning. Cultural empathy can be as simple as acknowledging how the external realities of the world impact the way someone feels. For example, I've worked with clients navigating the welfare system. When people tell me that the process has made them feel powerless, I might say to them, "I can hear that you're feeling powerless." That would be (the bare bones of) a "traditionally" empathetic approach.

But in order to culturally empathize with them, I might try to acknowledge in my response not only *what* they're feeling, but the *meaning* of what they're feeling: that they are being deliberately, cruelly disenfranchised by society. I might say something like, "I can hear that you're feeling powerless, which is really understandable, as you're navigating a system that strips you of your power." Responses like this, that add cultural weight to someone's emotions, can be extremely validating, and send the message that you not only see a person's emotions, but you see the invisible scaffolding of their reality.

Myira describes work she's done with people who are trapped in abusive relationships that they believe they cannot leave due to their cultural backgrounds and/or religious beliefs. When working with these clients, she says, she identifies themes such as a lack of autonomy or lack of control; she then encourages the client to reflect on where else in their life they might have experienced these themes (for example, as a marginalized person of color in a majority white society). She asks them to consider, "Where is that experience of an oppressive relationship being further reinforced by society?" This means taking her clients beyond just their feelings of sadness or isolation and instead grasping the full complexity of the power dynamics at play in their lives as minoritized women.

Adding this balloon weight to our empathy can help the person we're empathizing with to feel more held. It also sends the message that that person's feelings are not a problem or disorder that exists inside them, but part of a web that extends far beyond them. None of us are alone with our feelings; they spring from culture, relationships, and our place in society. There is something about this acknowledgment that has the potential to make someone feel less alone.

Another straightforward but crucial aspect of anti-oppressive empathy is simply communicating: "I believe you." This sounds basic enough, and yet it is astounding how often marginalized people's emotions are belittled in a society that trivializes their problems. Like a dismissive parent, the dominant culture might wag its finger at people and tell them, "It didn't happen that way," or "You're overreacting." The small, decent act of telling someone that their feelings are real, and you believe them, can itself be a radical way to empathize.

Sam Hope is an anti-oppressive counselor who is firmly of the opinion that believing someone's experiences is a fundamental aspect of empathy. Sam has been a person-centered counselor for over fifteen years, and also delivers training in anti-oppressive therapeutic work.* As a trans, autistic person, they describe feeling constantly invalidated by assumptions that they are "overreacting or overexaggerating" about things that are hurtful or overwhelming to them. This is clearly a barrier to empathy. "How do you connect to somebody's experience if you don't believe their experience?" Sam asks. They have also seen this in their work with abuse victims. We as a culture "collectively dissociate from abuse," says Sam. "People have created defenses in order to block their empathy." In other words, disbelieving people, or choosing not to engage with the terror they feel, can be a misguided way of trying to keep ourselves safe.

Another important element of empathizing, then, is

---

* Their book *Person-Centred Counselling for Trans and Gender Diverse People: A Practical Guide* is also a fantastic resource.

becoming aware of what our own defenses are that stop us from fully connecting to the horror and fear felt by others, so that we might let go of them and allow ourselves to connect. What are we afraid of? What are we burying our heads in the sand about? It's important that we do this, as Sam explains, because our defenses don't just keep us safe from icky, uncomfortable, or painful feelings. They also mean that we fail to challenge the structural power that leads to abuse in the first place. Silence and avoidance are complicity. "Charitably, we can say it's dissociation and a set of defenses," says Sam. "But effectively what it manages to do is maintain the status quo."

Transgender people have their realities constantly questioned and invalidated by the rampant transphobia that has dominated mainstream culture in the UK and the US in recent years. As the paranoid media whips up controversy with an endless stream of articles on hot-button topics like puberty blockers for teenagers and gendered bathrooms, the real issues that face trans people—like a lack of fair access to the mental and physical healthcare they desperately need—are ignored. To empathize with a transgender person fully, then, would mean listening to them nondefensively when they tell you about the issues that affect them the most. The actor Elliot Page has spoken about sharing articles with his mother to try and engender empathy for his experience as a trans man in America. "I think it's about sharing the correct information, because there are endless, full-blown lies about our lives, our healthcare, just who we are," he said.[17]

Page hits on why it's so important to believe marginalized people when they tell you what is impacting them—they are fighting against the brutal current of a world that trains us to be skeptical. But he also, implicitly, illustrates a third crucial component of anti-oppressive empathizing: that is, we shouldn't place the burden on people who are marginalized to educate those who are less so. Anti-oppressive practice teaches us that we should not expect marginalized people to educate us on their experiences before we can empathize with them. Instead, we should take it as our duty to educate ourselves.

This could sound contradictory. After all, I've spent most of this book telling you that you should always let someone tell you about their own life, rather than make assumptions about what's happening for them and how they feel about it. So how can we learn without asking people to teach us about themselves? These two things can be true at once: We can approach people with openness and humility, allowing them to teach us about their experiences, while also doing some of the legwork to understand the broader context, so that they don't have the burden of explaining it all to us. This could mean reading articles and books written by people from marginalized communities, watching TV shows or listening to podcasts, looking up terms and concepts you're unfamiliar with, and generally being open and curious to learn more about the world from perspectives other than the ones you're used to.

Empathy is radical

While this kind of research won't teach you about an individual's own unique life, it may give you a baseline grasp of key issues and concepts that impact them, before you speak to them about their specific experiences. If you're already approaching them with some knowledge, the person you're speaking to doesn't have to give you a full breakdown of, for example, the meaning of gender dysphoria before you are able to empathize with them about their experience of being misgendered.

In my own life, I've experienced what a relief this kind of informed empathy can be when, after my autism diagnosis, I began working with a therapist who had been trained in neurodiversity awareness. Previously, I'd found it hard to talk to counselors about my suspicions that I may be autistic. No matter how cherished and supported I felt by these wonderful counselors in other ways, when the subject of our sessions moved on to autism, I could sense their stiffening discomfort. Without broader knowledge of the different ways autistic traits can present beyond the widely known stereotypes, these counselors could not understand me. They would even gently challenge my need to "label myself." Talking to them about experiences like meltdowns felt impossible—for a start, I'd have to take up five minutes of our session to just explain what a meltdown even was. I found myself doing the mental calculations: At £60 per fifty-minute session, that meant paying £5 just to teach my counselor something. I didn't have the cash to spare.

Empathy Takes Action

Meeting a counselor who already understood concepts like "meltdowns" and "shutdowns" gave me the freedom to talk about my experiences—like talking to another autistic person, it gave me a shortcut to empathy. This allowed me to be more authentic in counseling, and to share more of what I was genuinely feeling. It made me feel safe—they didn't challenge my need to "label myself," but showed an implicit acceptance of my right to describe my own experience in the language that worked for me.

Making an effort to educate yourself is a form of empathy in action. Sometimes, just "feeling into" someone's experience is not enough. Empathy may require you to do more than feel. For Tyla, the content creator I spoke to, what's important in empathizing is not how people feel about your problems, but what people *do*. "I don't always need sympathy," she says. "I need action. I need you to do something."

In the counseling room, we can support a client practically as they battle systemic issues. This could mean working collaboratively with clients to move toward solutions or improve their situations, signposting clients toward services that can offer them more practical support, or sharing resources. It could even mean reducing your fees for a client who's lost their job, or allowing a client who is chronically ill to move their session time around to accommodate their flare-ups. There is debate in the counseling world about how much of a counselor's role is to advocate for their clients, but in many contexts where counselors work with very

Empathy is radical

vulnerable communities—such as abuse survivors or refugees—it's common to hear of therapists who take practical action on behalf of their clients, making referrals and writing supportive letters to other professionals.

Outside of the counseling room, socially and culturally aware empathy can be the fuel that drives you to take action. It's this action that communicates your empathy to others. Whether it's taking part in a protest for an issue that does not directly affect you, offering free childcare, or taking the time to educate yourself about others' experiences—the action is the empathy.

If, on your way to work, you see a person who is experiencing homelessness asking for money or food, you might feel pity. It is kind to recognize someone's distress and to feel for them—but it also keeps them beneath you. Instead, empathy might bring you to consider how the housing crisis, spiraling cost of living, structural racism, and other big-picture social factors may have led that person to where they are today. You might see the person's need in the context of the society that has shaped their situation. You might acknowledge them rather than turn away, listen attentively to their story, and believe it. You might commit to learning more about the homelessness crisis in your city, and you might consider how you can use your position of relative privilege to give a little power back to that person and others in their shoes—perhaps by putting some money in their hands or joining your local renters' union or anti-eviction protest. Empathy does not drive you to do any of this because it makes you feel like a good person, but because really empathizing with others who are in more marginalized positions than yours means taking steps to redistribute power.

Surrendering power

In a famous exchange on the 2017 season of the UK reality dating show *Love Island*, two contestants who were dating got into an unexpected discussion about women's rights.

"Surely you believe in equality?" Camilla asked, aghast at her partner Jonny's scoffing about feminism.

"Oh, I believe in equality," Jonny retorted, "but I feel like feminism believes in, almost, *inequality*."

The interaction is a perfect everyday example of the idea that when you are accustomed to privilege, equality feels like oppression. Sacrificing a little of your own power to someone with less is only tipping the scales back to where they should be: a steady equilibrium. But when you're the one falling from the higher position, you might feel only the sinking sensation of the drop.

These power dynamics show up in the practice of empathy, too. People with more privilege have their own points of view reinforced and validated constantly, and are scarcely asked to consider the points of view of people with less. To take one pervasive example, if you're cisgender, your name and pronouns are likely to be easily and effortlessly used by people around you day-to-day, without you needing to correct or remind them. If you have an English name in an English-speaking culture, it's likely that others correctly pronounce your name more often than not. When you're corrected on your pronunciation or asked to use they/them pronouns by others, it might feel onerous to you—like you are being asked to do extra work to make someone feel comfortable. But in fact, you are only attempting to give others the same level of comfort that you're already experiencing by default.

As bell hooks once wrote in her quest to define love, "We cannot know love if we remain unable to surrender our attachment to power."[18] The same is true of empathy. Forging real connections means not bitterly clinging to our own power, guarding it like a knight posted at the gates of a fortress, but instead acknowledging, sharing, and relinquishing it. This doesn't always feel good. The needs of others might clang loudly as they crash against your tightly held shield. Think of the blustering, defensive figure of Jonny from *Love Island*, who, in being asked to consider that some women might like to have more rights, seems to believe that such women are specifically attacking *his* rights.

I think of the men who, in stark contrast to Jonny, have made me, as a woman, feel empathized with throughout my life. There are the male friends who have taken the time to listen to my experiences of sexual harassment and not played "devil's advocate" by imagining what the harasser might have intended, nor asked too many questions about *why* what I experienced was harassment. There are the male colleagues who have shared their salaries with me and encouraged me to negotiate for the same. And there is the first psychotherapist I went to see long-term, who, after I had disclosed historical abuse to him, asked me, "What is it like to talk about this with me, as a man?"

His question stunned me so much that I wasn't sure how to answer. I was not used to men acknowledging their own role of power in their relationships with me. I was used to men who unthinkingly wielded that power—those who might have told me that what happened to me wasn't so bad, or questioned whether I was telling the truth. I was even used to men who would express pity or effusive praise, in a way that shored up their own view of themselves as *one of the good ones*. One such man was once so horrified by an experience I shared with him that I found myself comforting *him* with reassurances.

This therapist, however, chose instead to name the difference between us and ask how it impacted our relationship. Ten years later, at beginning of my own career as a therapist, I understand more profoundly the intent behind his question. He was deliberately drawing attention to the power dynamic between us and redressing it by inviting me to share my experience of it with him. Had it been scarier to talk freely with him than it might be with another woman? Had I self-censored, biting my tongue rather than letting him hear the full extent of my pain? Had I stopped myself from getting angry, played the "good victim"?

Empathy is radical

Inviting me to consider these questions deepened my trust in this therapist. It showed that he was willing to talk about my experiences in a way that many men would avoid, uncomfortable with confronting their own quiet privilege. His commitment to empathy was greater than his commitment to holding on to power. Rather than standing guard at the castle gates, he was walking forward to meet me on the bridge over the moat.

6

Empathy is work

Sometimes, in a counseling session, empathy fails. It can take only a second. Perhaps a client goes somewhere I struggle to follow. They might be deliberately trying to lose me, afraid of what I'll see if I get too close. Perhaps I suggest an exercise or make an interpretation that jars with the client; their hackles go up. The client says something crucial in passing and it slips through my fingers like smoke. In these moments, something is missed, and we move further apart.

With Tony, this happened over and over. For several sessions, we just couldn't grasp each other. Tony was a tower of a young man, who had a way of speaking that was viscerally descriptive, flecked with blood and sweat and tears. He intimidated me. I found myself internally cowering a little whenever he spoke, in particular, about his younger brother, Harry. Although he had begun by speaking about issues totally unrelated to his brother, as we unspooled the thread of his story, Tony kept coming back to complaints about Harry. No one could irritate Tony like Harry. He was full of criticisms about the younger man: He was sniveling, weak, pathetic, overemotional, needy, naive. No matter how many methods I tried to keep our sessions focused on Tony himself, disdainful remarks about his brother would somehow always work their way in.

Each time Tony unleashed a new tirade about his brother, I found myself imagining the bowed, sorrowful figure of Harry, my empathy extending to the younger brother rather than the client sat before me. I was acutely aware that my job here was to empathize with Tony—but, as he hid behind this wall of insults, I struggled to find him. This was no accident. The way that I was feeling in these sessions with Tony was a kind of "countertransference." This is a psychoanalytical term that essentially describes the emotions that clients provoke in therapists. I wondered if my fear of Tony was a reaction that he commonly induced in others, and whether that might be something he was doing subconsciously to protect himself. Did it keep him safe, to hide behind his criticisms and violent deflections? Were his judgments of his brother a way of avoiding being judged himself?

This work with Tony came at the beginning of my

psychotherapy career, when I was carrying a lot of self-doubt. I struggled with the feeling that I wasn't "getting it right." I believed I should always be harmoniously empathizing with my clients. I started to really grow as a therapist when I accepted that, occasionally, getting it wrong is part of the point. The important thing is that, when I lose my client along the trail, I don't stop trying to find them. I make it my responsibility to show that I am by their side. If something is ugly, difficult, or uncomfortable, we face it together. For Tony, I realized, it was important that despite my inability to grasp him, I was still reaching out my hands and trying.

Many of us have been wounded in our lives by the failure of someone close to us to really show up as we needed them to. In therapy, we have an opportunity to experience someone else's true commitment to understanding life from our perspective, no matter how challenging it gets. I have learned from psychotherapy that good empathetic relationships are based in effort. In fact, sometimes the empathy *is* the effort. When we don't immediately comprehend something, we keep trying to understand. When the terrain gets steep and rocky, we put on our climbing shoes.

Back in the 1950s, the psychoanalyst Erich Fromm wrote that love "is a constant challenge; it is not a resting place, but a moving, growing, working together"; "it isn't a feeling, it is a practice." Fromm's treatise, *The Art of Loving*, spelled out how love requires discipline, faith, patience, and is an artform that must be learned in the same way that we learn any other.[1] I believe that the same is true of empathy: that it is not a quality that you may or may not possess, but a skill that we all must practice and develop over the course of our lives, but also in every new relationship we build with every person we meet. The work is forever ongoing.

Throughout this book, we've contemplated some of the core principles of empathy, and from each of these principles emerges a guideline for how to practice it. Empathy doesn't assume, and so we must meet others humbly. Empathy is an embodied process, so we need to feel safe in our own bodies and get in touch with our own emotions to be able to fully experience it. Empathy is amoral—it's not about performing goodness or judging who is good enough to receive it—so we must leave our judgments at the door. Empathy is radical, and so necessitates redressing power imbalances. The final pillar of empathy is one that underpins all of the others: Empathy is work. Empathy does not occur automatically, but through our commitment to working toward it, no matter the obstacles.

I want to end this book by talking about some of the most important things I've learned—and unlearned—about how to work at empathy, and what that might look like in practice. Forget about empathy as the personality trait of "nice" people; forget about the empathy that is really a synonym for sympathy, pity, or kindness; forget about empathy that looks like politeness, or following social norms. Forget about empathy as an unconscious impulse, something you either feel for someone or you don't. Empathy is a muscle, and any of us—no matter our starting strength—can put it to work.

Learning and unlearning empathy

After several circular, frustrating sessions, I decided to try something new with Tony. As he spoke about a childhood incident between him and his brother that he'd mentioned several times before, I suggested that we try something called chair work. Chair work, or "the empty chair," is an idea from the Gestalt school of psychotherapy—one of the kinds of therapy that I sometimes draw on in my practice. Gestalt therapy is all about what's affecting us in the here-and-now and being rooted in the moment. Gestalt therapists use empty chairs to encourage clients to connect with whatever it is that's looming large for them. We bring an empty, third chair into the therapy space, and together, we imagine that there is a presence sitting in the chair—whether that's a past self, a future self, or perhaps a family member who is living or dead. By speaking directly to the chair, the client may be able to get in touch with parts of themselves they might not be able to reach by speaking to the therapist alone.

Tony and I agreed to imagine that his brother was sitting in the empty chair—the child version of his brother, at the age of the incident between them that we'd just been discussing. Initially Tony was, as I could have predicted, dismissive toward his imagined brother. He insulted the invisible child sitting in the chair and kept his face turned coldly away from him.

But as he continued speaking to his child brother—with gentle encouragement from me to keep digging deeper—something began to shift. Tony's body started to seem more childlike itself. He twisted in his seat, his limbs suddenly bending with the elasticity of a seven-year-old's. He chewed the inside of his cheek. His eyes softened. For perhaps the first time, he didn't intimidate me at all. He seemed small, shy, and afraid.

Catching this glimpse of Tony as a child brought me closer into his world. I felt something of his hurt and confusion as a small boy, and it began to make a kind of sense to me how this hurt had metastasized into vitriol for his brother. I began to see what was behind all of Tony's ironclad defenses: a small, scared boy who just wanted to be safe and loved. This helped me to make sense of Tony's anger—there was a part of him that was neglected, and the devastation of this neglect had found an outlet in hatred. In future sessions, Tony and I continued to lose each other—like most things in relationships, building empathy is not linear. But it became easier for me to work my way back toward Tony by holding on to the image of the young child who hid inside this posturing young man. The boy lurked in the corner of Tony's gaze, pigeon-toed and soft-eyed.

Empathy is work

Empathy often comes more easily when we manage to make contact with someone's most vulnerable self, which usually, in my experience, contains an echo of their child self. Perhaps it's because this is something that's common to all of us—that we were all once children. Seeing the child in someone else touches the child in us, and so touches on our common humanity. It might also be because children have an innate capacity for empathy that is corroded and distorted by the process of growing up, when we learn all the normative and deflective ways of being that keep us separate from one another (and so, safe from one another). The child version of ourselves is the version from before the world taught us to mask; in other words, to defensively guard ourselves against being vulnerable, as Tony did. These are ways that we learn to survive. They are also ways that we maintain the space between ourselves and others.

Childhood may be a time when empathy comes easily; it is also a vital time for learning the skills we need to connect with others. There has been plenty of recent research into how empathy develops in children, demonstrating that measurable traits of empathy are often shaped by the environment a child grows up in, with home lives, school lives, and friendships all shown to play a crucial role. Some researchers have focused on parenting, with one 2011 study suggesting that parents who emphasize the importance of taking other people's perspectives and generally take a sensitive and responsive approach to parenting are more likely to raise empathetic children.*[2] Others have taken a broader approach, noting that warm, supportive parents are one element of a bigger picture, along with solid friendships and positive relationships with teachers, which have all been shown to have a positive impact on young people's abilities to show empathetic behaviors. Meanwhile, those who have faced mental health challenges at a young age have been shown to be less likely to demonstrate empathy.[3]

Though all the usual caveats apply to these studies that claim to measure empathy, there is a general sense that we all start learning at young ages how to treat one another, and how to be in relation with each other, and growing up in a traumatic environment may hinder this learning process. As we touched on in chapter 3, trauma experienced in childhood can linger in your body for the rest of your life. The worlds that surround us as small children directly shape who we are. A 2015 study drew a clear link between being prey to bullying or victimization as a child and having "lower empathy."[4] This doesn't mean that children who are bullied are callous or cold, but that children who have been victimized by their peers or the people who are

---

* It's not my intention here to echo the offensive and outdated idea of "refrigerator parents." Back in the 1950s, some academics blamed parents for their children's diagnoses of autism, suggesting that autistic traits were a result of "cold" parenting. Parents are not responsible for their children's diagnoses. But equally, parenting is an important thread in the densely woven fabric of a child's life, and how we're parented indelibly shapes who we are. I believe that, in this sense, how we're parented is part of what shapes how we empathize and relate to one another.

Empathy is work

supposed to care for them are less likely to show "empathy" in the traditional sense. They might keep themselves wrapped up and shielded, closely guarding their wounds. They might learn to lash out and hurt others before getting hurt themselves. They might exist in a state of fight-or-flight.

When talking about empathy, we have to embrace some contradictory ideas. So, yes, empathy is a conscious process that we begin learning as children. The work of active listening, of moving toward one another, is an effortful exercise that we can all embark on. But there is another aspect of empathy, an unselfconscious openness and humility, a willingness to be wrong, that is less a matter of learning than it is of unlearning. Children may, in fact, be better at it than adults, who have spent a lifetime guarding themselves against vulnerability.

Practicing empathy is a matter of both learning and unlearning. What follows are some tools and principles I've learned about empathy from my research and practice of it, both inside and outside of the therapy room. That being said, tools and principles will take us only so far. Empathizing is also about connecting to your imaginative, playful, and curious senses. Relating to people is a slightly different experience every time. The kind of empathy that works for one person will not work for another, and the way you practice empathy might not be the way I practice it. Empathy is a shape-shifter.

This paradox is one that therapists in training grapple

with. Our training gives us an ethical framework, an overview of historical and contemporary theories about the human condition, and a heap of experience in active listening and forming connections. But it does not churn out therapists who all empathize in the same way—at the end of the course, the therapists travel off in infinite different directions, developing practices and relationships that look entirely different from one another. Even within my own work as a therapist, I experience every new relationship with each new client as its own little world. From the generations of psychotherapists that came before us, we learn soft guiding principles to empathy, carved out like desire paths that flatten grass. But there are no signposts, no maps. We find our own way, each and every time.

Lessons from psychotherapy

Some of the core lessons from psychotherapy about practicing empathy can be helpful in any relationship. These include listening for the emotions underneath someone's words; checking that you're understanding them correctly and working through any knots in communication; reflecting feelings; allowing plentiful space for tears; and asking open questions. Crucially, psychotherapy also teaches that true empathy necessitates true authenticity. You can experience real connection only when you're being your real self—and so, if being your real self means adapting or letting go of any of the traditional facets of "empathy," such as making eye contact, then so be it. It's more important that you are genuine.

One of the most critical tools in practicing empathy is listening for emotions. In a culture of intellectualizing and moralizing—a culture indelibly shaped by the oppressive forces of white supremacy and capitalism—our emotions are often obscured or sidelined. When we're tearfully ranting about a partner's inability to clean up after themself, or raging about an injustice we read about in the news, a good therapist listens for the emotions that underlie the content of our words. An even better therapist tries to connect us to those emotions more fully. There's good reason for the cliché that therapists will always ask you: "And how did that make you feel?"

By always following the thread of someone's emotions, we can find at the other end a more vulnerable version of them, like I did with Tony. For me, this has been the key to empathizing: always searching for the beating heart that is resonating through someone's story. Therapy is a precious space for empathy because it allows us the time and attention to really get under the surface of an issue and search for its emotional core in this way. We can take it beyond analyzing the rights and wrongs of what happened, and instead really sit with the feelings that might be unwanted or feel too shameful to share elsewhere.

Another one of my most-used questions in the therapy room is: "Have I got that right?" I normally ask this after I take a swing at interpreting the aches and anxieties that I hear pulsating through a client's words. Rather than tell them how I think they're feeling, I like to continually check how well my listening is aligning with their reality. Sometimes, they tell me that I've got it wrong. Clients may get angry or frustrated when it's clear that our perspectives on a situation have diverged. Occasionally, we hit a bump in the road of our relationship. This might be due to the same tricky relationship patterns that the client faces in their life trickling into the therapy. Or it could simply be that I've made a mistake. When this happens, as it inevitably does, all is not lost. Mistakes and ruptures are an opportunity to get even closer, by working hard to get back on to the same page.

Inside or outside the therapy room, repairing a fracture in a relationship can take many different forms. It might mean, again, listening out for the unmet needs or unexpressed emotions that are beneath someone's anger and trying to speak to them. It might mean allowing two emotional realities to coexist, even when you deeply disagree with the other person's point of view, or if it painfully clashes with your own. It might mean relaxing the high standards you are used to holding yourself and others to, and exercising forgiveness and compassion. What's important in these instances is not the specifics of how we attempt to repair our conflicts, but the fact that we show up to do so.

Another fundamental aspect of empathy is reflection: the basic active listening skill that everyone learns at the

Empathy is work

onset of their counseling training. Reflection is the practice of making yourself a mirror. Having heard their emotion, you acknowledge it back to them. In practice, this usually just means naming the feeling. Someone might unravel a story about their neighbors having aggressive, loud fights on the other side of their wall, for example, and after listening to their trembling account, I might say, "It sounds like you're feeling afraid." It sounds incredibly simple, and that's because it is. But it's also a lot more difficult than you might think. A large amount of therapeutic training is just learning how to hone this skill of identifying and naming emotions—with as much accuracy as possible, but also with a willingness to get it wrong. It's always better to take a shot, after all, than to leave someone feeling unheard. If you're wrong, they can tell you, "No, I'm not afraid exactly. . . . I'm feeling angry." This opens the door for even more exploration, and crucially, it also gives you another opportunity to reflect with, "I can hear your anger."

Once we've successfully identified and reflected someone's emotions, we can move on to another vital step in the empathetic process: making space for those feelings. In day-to-day life, when someone cries, many of us rush to say some version of "Don't cry!" This sends the message that we're uncomfortable with seeing someone hurt, and that we need them to express themself differently. As a therapist, when someone cries in front of me, I acknowledge the tears and the sadness they represent, and I hit the brakes on the pace of the session. Tears are to be sat with; feelings are to be felt. When we quietly and calmly allow someone to cry, scream, wail, or whatever they may need in the moment, rather than shushing or rushing them, we're being more empathetic because we're showing that their emotional reality is accepted, and that it's safe to feel however they feel. Silence can sometimes be the most empathetic expression of all.

We can also intentionally ask questions in a more empathetic way. I lead with curiosity, not with assumptions or presupposed narratives—which means making sure that my questions are as open and broad as possible. I try to ask, "Can you tell me more about how that feels?," not "Do you feel lonely?" Questions should throw open doors of possibility, giving the person answering plenty of space to wander around as they sort through their thoughts and feelings. A closed question—one that invites an answer of "yes" or "no"—can be an emotional slam of the door.

If I'm not able to ask someone questions about their experience directly, I might instead ask myself some questions to foster empathy. I consider: What is the feeling under this person's words or actions? What is the unmet need that they're expressing? What are the broader social structures that might be impacting them? How might their culture, life experiences, or trauma be shaping the way they're acting?

For me, these are the most important lessons from my therapy work about how to practice empathy: to always listen closely for emotions, helping the person to connect more deeply with their own feelings. To use silence and contain my own reactions to create a generous amount of space for that person to express their feelings. To ask questions that open up more space, more possibilities, rather than imposing any narratives or assumptions of my own. Above all, to believe each person's account of their own experience, and to be a reliable and steadfast witness to it. These principles and skills have served me well in learning how to better communicate and practice empathy. But empathy itself is something greater than the sum of learning how to ask open questions, hold silences, and name people's feelings.

Perhaps the most fundamental element of practicing empathy is authenticity: It's possible to connect with someone else's truest self, and the truest expression of their feelings, only when they're also comfortable connecting with that truest self and you're comfortable connecting with your own. As Carl Rogers himself observed, "in relationships with persons I have found that it does not help, in the long run, to act as though I were something I am not."[5] We have to be able to be fully genuine in order to really connect with others. This genuineness cannot reliably be found in the scripts and stereotypes that are taught to us by society. In fact, studying how to be more "empathetic" might just be teaching us new parts to play, new dance steps to follow, new masks we can wear that take us further away from ourselves and others.

Lessons from neurodiversity

One of the biggest examples of the narrow scope of "empathy" in counseling is the emphasis on eye contact. In my own training, we were taught the importance of staring into a client's eyes from day one. This is highly neuronormative—in other words, it's something that neurotypical people might find normal and reassuring, but many neurodivergent people struggle with. To be frank, I'd probably struggle to make consistent eye contact with my own spouse on my wedding day, let alone with a stranger for a fifty-minute counseling session. And yet, on the very first day of my psychotherapy training, my tutors instructed the group to wordlessly greet everybody else in the room using only our eyes. Before many of us—twenty-four awkward-elbowed strangers—had ever spoken a word to one another, we circled the room, nodding and smiling shyly as we met one another's gaze.

Looking back, I don't remember much about these encounters, other than the mental energy I was expending to make sure I met each person's gaze. In my mind, the exercise was something more akin to playing darts than it was a meeting of minds. I was trying, with extreme effort, to hit the targets.

As an autistic person, my relationship with eye contact is a queer one. An inability to make eye contact is among the most well-known signifiers of autism. I wouldn't describe myself as totally unable to make eye contact. I physically can do it, and I've felt its power, its nakedness: a wordless glance held over a drink in the fourth hour of a date; a hesitant look as someone pauses for breath while unspooling the dark thread of a secret. But—perhaps because of this very intimacy—I've also struggled with it. I'm told that I have a way of "working up to" eye contact when I'm talking with someone, my gaze landing carefully on their cheekbone, their jaw, their hairline, before eventually meeting their eyes. Sometimes, I consciously notice myself doing this, such as when I'm ordering coffee: I'll deliberately look just past a barista's eyes, smiling widely, trying to dispense the necessary amount of friendly eye contact in the same mechanical way that they are dispensing my flat white.

Therapists are taught to believe that what we see in a client's eyes—in some cases, above and beyond what they actually say—is their truth, and that a lack of willingness to make eye contact might itself represent something significant. But for an autistic person, the deepest moments of connection don't necessarily involve eye contact. I've had some of the most vulnerable conversations of my life while driving or walking side-by-side. I prefer situations where I can comfortably be alongside someone, not staring into one another, but collaboratively moving along the same path. As a therapist, I sometimes feel despondent that even the very set-up of counseling—two people facing one another in chairs—is neuronormative. In a world that constantly tries to force autistic people to meet its gaze and forces misinterpretations on their meandering eyes, a therapist might most effectively empathize with them by, in fact, looking away.

A new wave of neurodivergent therapists are beginning to challenge the ways that empathy is taught. It's increasingly common for therapists to offer outdoor therapy, in which they take a walk alongside clients, breaking the mold of the two-chair therapy process and its unrelenting eye contact. The spirit of neurodiversity recognizes that everyone is different and needs different things—so therapy shouldn't be trying to impose some idea of "normality" on us, to bring us more in line with social norms. Instead, it should embrace our differences, allowing us to empathize more deeply as we meet each other as our truest selves.

The spirit of neurodiversity is also about unlearning the ideas that have been taught to us by the dominant, neuronormative culture. In a 2023 article, the psychologist Matthew J. Bolton argued that the best way to treat autistic clients is to stop learning so much about how to treat autistic clients. I've spoken previously about the need to educate ourselves on different neurotypes, backgrounds, and cultures, and how transformative it's been for me personally when I worked with a therapist who was neurodiversity-aware. I agree with Bolton, however, that this textbook knowledge needs to be held lightly. "Pre-conceived knowledge applied too rigidly can be damaging," he writes. "Experiential learning in being-with real, nonlinear persons—not merely in the presence of the clean, clinical labels which attempt to describe them—is indispensable to psychological contact."[6] No textbook can replace the information gained from getting to know a person and being in their presence. Simply being yourself and allowing others to be themselves, however that might look for them, can take you a long way.

One idea that can help us in this work is standpoint theory. Academics Robert Chapman and Monique Botha argue that, when it comes to empathizing with neurodivergent people in therapy, we need to recognize that people in marginalized positions in society have access to knowledge that people in privileged positions don't have (that is, each of us has a different view from our "standpoint"). Chapman and Botha note that historically, in the medical model of autism, autistic people have been viewed as "lacking in insight and self-awareness in relation to neurotypical experts."[7] This has led to an environment in therapy where autistic people have felt that their neurotypical therapists were not empathetic toward them, despite apparently having a lot of "knowledge" about autism. A study by Sonny Hallett (who I chatted to in chapter 1) and fellow psychotherapist Colin Kerr found that "autism specialism amongst practitioners often [isn't] a guarantee of positive experiences, and in fact may lead to the opposite if outdated or inaccurate information about autism was being used."[8]

Though these studies look specifically at the experiences of autistic people in psychotherapy, they can teach us all something about how to work at empathy. Primarily, they highlight the sense of humility that is innate to empathy—meaning that you're never really done with learning how to empathize. Each new person can teach you something new. Being empathetic means always approaching both others with a willingness to learn and the world with questions. Without these challenges, these reframings, these reimaginings, we will not be able to overcome the social barriers that keep us apart from one another. As the psychologist and author of the groundbreaking book *Decolonizing Therapy*, Dr. Jennifer Mullan, once said: "If we don't lovingly get curious about how we've been trained, there is no room for possibility of change."[9] Her framing of curiosity as an act of love is deeply resonant. This is true not only for therapists, but for all of us. If we choose to stay on the surface level of our world and not get curious about what lies beneath, we can never truly get close to one another.

In keeping with standpoint theory, I've found that in my conversations with autistic people for this book, their wisdom on empathy has been reflected back to me, time and time again. In my conversation with the neurodivergent biochemist Camilla Pang, she told me that she takes umbrage with the idea that there's one particular way to show empathy. It has always annoyed her, she explains, that people who express affection or warmth in a socially acceptable way might be viewed as being "more" empathetic than others. "You don't have to hug to be empathetic," she muses. "It's like sustainability. People think, 'If I recycle, I'm going to be sustainable. If I hug someone, I'm going to be empathetic.'" But this way of looking at it is too simplistic; too gestural. "The whole process of empathy is knowing that it presents differently in different people. You have to meet people where they are."

Empathy is an inherently imaginative and expansive process: It makes space for someone else's reality within your reality. It fights against the constrictive straitjackets of cultural norms and stereotypes, and it dares to imagine something new. In this sense, it is a paradigm shift. It's not about following a set of rules, but accepting that there are no fixed rules. It's antihierarchical and liberatory. It follows that we can learn as much about empathy from activists, leaders, and rebels within our communities as we can from therapists like me, who were trained by institutions and textbooks.

What we learn from each other

I've experienced profound empathy through being in community with other disabled people. From the disability justice movement, I've learned the importance of recognizing how interconnected systems like ableism and white supremacy divide and confine us, and how emancipatory work that fights against these systems can be acts of love and empathy. Perhaps most importantly, I've seen the wisdom of empathy that exists innately in care work and community.

Disability justice was born from a "second wave" of the disability rights movement in the twenty-first century, and is a movement led by disabled people of color and queer and transgender disabled people. One of its most prominent thinkers, the artist, author, and activist Patty Berne, writes in a radical call-to-arms, "We are in a global system that is incompatible with life. There is no way to stop a single gear in motion—we must dismantle this machine."[10]

Berne's words reflect the radical spirit of empathy that we explored in chapter 5. Dismantling the machine within all of us might mean confronting the biases and assumptions we hold, the stereotypes and prejudices that stop us from empathizing with one another, and working to demolish power structures in our interactions with other people. The world we live in shapes how we empathize with one another. Under capitalism, we are incentivized to commodify and objectify each other, seeing people in terms of their "worth," whether that's the amount of money they have, how attractive they are, or how much social power they hold. We're driven to compete with each other—for jobs, money, resources—in a way that is anathema to empathy. Not to mention, the simple reality of trying to exist in a capitalist society leaves us running on fumes, often too burnt out to really work on our relationships with each other. As the writer Sophia K. Rosa puts it in her 2022 book *Radical Intimacy*, "Most people struggle under capitalism to locate enough time and energy to nurture relationships at all.... It is a devastating reality that so much of our lifeforce is directed towards labor, rather than love."[11]

"Compassion fatigue" is an idea that's frequently discussed in the medical field, particularly among nurses. The constant demand for care and compassion—particularly on overstuffed and understaffed wards, circuses of trauma and desperate need—can calcify into a sense of numbness. There is only so much a person is capable of giving. Therapists sometimes struggle with compassion fatigue, too, and we must be conscious of where our personal limits are. There's always a risk, if you try to support too many clients, that it will affect your ability to be empathetic and build good relationships with them. In fact, it's part of the British Association for Counselling and Psychotherapy (or BACP) ethical framework as a core duty of our profession to take care of ourselves as practitioners.[12] By this, the BACP doesn't mean that we must take baths and use face masks—it means that we must be conscious of not stretching ourselves too thin, so that we don't run the risk of burning through our supplies of empathy.

I've also noticed compassion fatigue appearing in my clients when they are under particular stress or dealing with immense trauma of their own. This may be expressed sideways, in the form of cruelty, coldness, or an unsympathetic take on a friend or relative—like my client Tony's vitriol toward his younger brother. Often, when someone is failing to understand (or not putting the work into understanding) someone else in this way, it's because they're battling the raw pain of an unmet need themself. They are being deprived of something, or stretched far beyond the limits of what they can materially cope with. Their response is to self-protectively shut down—the work it would take to really connect is too much to bear, so they distance themselves instead.

In short, for many people, our society is dangerous and draining. This is not always a conducive environment in which to work on relating to others. Fighting to "dismantle the machine" of these social systems can, itself, be a loving act of empathy. One person whose activism is fueled by profound empathy is the disabled activist Damon Kirsebom. Damon is a nonspeaking autistic self-advocate based in Canada, who has produced several informative short films that have spread globally on YouTube, raising awareness of his experiences as a nonspeaking person. In one video, titled *Reframing Severe Autism*, Damon takes aim at the institutional, established framing of what it means to have "severe autism," arguing that the juxtaposition of "mild" versus "severe" autism is an oversimplification—and one that underestimates the capacity of people like him who are believed to be "severe." "I do understand the world around me," says a voiceover in the video reading Damon's words. "I have empathy for others.... Just by observing me, however, you will miss knowing what's in my mind."[13]

Empathy is work

Speaking to me over email, Damon explains that his journey into advocacy and activism has been one motivated at its core by empathy. It began for him when researching the history of disabled students' experiences in education led him to a deeply human feeling: *I'm not alone.* He saw his own experiences reflected in the lives of others and felt moved to take action. "Empathy, for me, is the reason I advocate," says Damon. "I care deeply about the way injustices negatively affect the wellbeing of others. The greatest barrier to empathy, in my experience, is the unwillingness to question existing paradigms about autism. Understanding leads to acceptance, it seems; therefore, wanting to understand is necessary for mutual empathy." For Damon, the liberating work of raising awareness and challenging dominant narratives about autism is as important for empathy as cultivating interpersonal skills. Because empathy isn't just about the way we show up individually—it's about the world that surrounds us, the ideas that populate our minds, the lenses we view other people through.

Another key lesson from the disability justice movement is that—despite burnout or compassion fatigue or whatever you might call the exhaustion of facing the daily grind of oppression—disabled people and other marginalized people have a unique, lived expertise when it comes to care. In the seminal text *Care Work: Dreaming Disability Justice*, the activist and writer Leah Piepzna-Samarasinha sums this up with the idea of "crip emotional intelligence":

the notion that disabled people have our own, heightened form of emotional intelligence.[14] She notes that some people might find this idea challenging, because in an ableist society, it's rare to hear the admission that disabled people can be *better* at anything than abled people. But in fact, disabled and chronically ill people may be better practiced at giving each other grace and compassion. Among other things, Piepzna-Samarasinha defines crip emotional intelligence as "not taking it personally sometimes, when another disabled person is short with you, is fumbling for words, is frustrated." She also writes about the importance of noticing each other's signs of pain and overwhelm, of continuing to include people even when they cancel plans, of letting go of standard ableist expectations about things like work and fitness, and "never assuming. Anything."[15]

This concept of "crip emotional intelligence" is not just about being kinder to one another, but about being able to live in community and achieving interdependence. Counter to the independence championed by capitalist society and the disability rights movement, disability justice believes in interdependence: being able to depend on and care for one another. This vision of interdependence is one where no one is confined to institutions, but instead the community is able to "meet each others' needs as we build toward liberation."[16] It's a call for attunement to one another; for compassion, kindness, love. It's also about survival. Interdependence recognizes that we need each other—that relationships are perhaps the most powerful tool we have to "dismantle the machine."

Whether you're disabled or not, we can all learn some crucial lessons about empathy from the disability justice movement, and from the people supporting one another at the sharpest edges of society.* How to get closer to one another and build authentic connections can be learned from the bottom up, even more so than from the top down: Rather than listen only to the "experts" in empathy, we can also recognize the inherent wisdom about care and love that exists in our own communities. We can read all the books on empathy, watch all the lectures, and learn all the active listening skills under the sun—but the greatest resource we have to learn from is each other. There is no one correct way to practice empathy. Empathy is something we each make up together. In many ways, it's child's play.

Empathy heals

We cannot read each other's minds or know directly what's inside each other's hearts. Instead, it is how hard we work to understand each other that truly makes us human. Empathy is not an individualist act of telepathy. It's about connecting and resonating with other people rather than "reading" or assessing them. It allows us to experience our

---

* In this spirit, I have put together a reading list of works that have taught me a great deal about empathy, compiled at the end of this book.

common humanity. To me, this idea of empathy is generative and exciting. No one can be left out of it, just as no human can be left out of love. It's a concept as diverse and heterogenous as people themselves, and so it wouldn't make sense to say that any person is "deficient" or lacking in it. It's an evolving creative project: There are as many ways to empathize as there are people in the world. If we let go of empathy's traditional definition—the egocentric ability to "read" each other and perform societal norms—and instead embrace its infinite flexibility, then the possibilities for profound connection are unlimited.

There is no easy way to "do" empathy, and no one way to make sure you always get it right. All of us will fail at it sometimes. This, too, is being human: We fluctuate in and out of connection with one another, sometimes clanging as we collide, our perspectives and plural points of view coming into conflict. These dissonant moments are also opportunities for empathy. When we misunderstand each other, we have an opportunity to learn more about *how* to understand each other next time. Empathy isn't always soft and comforting. It can be confronting. It shows you where the gaps are between you and others. It shows you what you don't understand.

While it may not be one, straightforward process that we can excel in, there is one thing I'm sure of about empathy. No matter what it looks like, and no matter how it is offered, I believe in genuine empathy's power to heal. Of course, as a psychotherapist, I have to. But beyond therapy, connection with other people is something that we all need—all of us—in order to grow, survive, and thrive. No matter our experiences, our diagnoses, or our beliefs, we all need relationships with others, in whatever form that takes for us. Being seen and heard is what can lift us out of our personal despair. On a structural level, our solidarity with others is also what can liberate, unite, and soothe us under the harmful systems that oppress us.

Over the course of two years, I had many recorded and unrecorded conversations with people for this book. I asked most of them to share with me an experience that they'd had of "true empathy"—a moment in life when they'd felt really seen, understood, held. This question was repeatedly met with a sigh of frustration: As we struggled, together, to pick apart the cat's cradle of what empathy really was, we found ourselves tied in knots. (Here, you might think back to your own attempt to write your definition of empathy in chapter 1.) More than one interviewee responded to my question with a question, "What is *true empathy*, anyway?"

Some spoke of best friends who had noticed, across the candlelit chatter of a dinner party, that they were having a bad time, and found a way to intervene; friends who knew when to follow them out of rooms discreetly, to console them in private. Some spoke of family members or partners who were able to sit with them in perfect silence. Others noted times when broken cars, fridges, or laptops were fixed for them—when action was unhesitatingly taken, problems practically resolved without a trace of resentment. More than one person mentioned their therapist—usually, a moment from a therapy session when the therapist had astutely identified a deeper subtext to something they were saying.

Throughout these conversations, I tried to come up with my own answer. When had I experienced true empathy? I tried to clear my mind of any philosophizing or intellectualizing on the question of what empathy really is, and to listen to my gut: What came up for me when I pictured empathy in its purest form?

In the memory, I'm eight years old and wearing a green-and-white-checked school dress over scratchy woolen tights. I'm new to my school, having moved house a few months ago, and I'm still getting used to the way the uniform sits on my skin. Some things are familiar—I still bring the same white-bread-and-ham sandwiches in the same lunch box, to a cafeteria that feels like a similar wide mouth of cacophonous sound. But a lot is different. I've tentatively made two friends: Poppy and Sarah. I spend every lunch time with them, tracing circles around the playground as we walk its periphery. Besides them, I've struggled to get to know anyone else in my class. Everybody seems to have their groups already, to be swimming relentlessly forward in a current that I can't quite catch.

One afternoon, I'm walking home from school with Poppy. Sarah goes in the other direction, because she lives on a different side of town. Suddenly, in the middle of chatting about something else, Poppy reaches out and touches my forearm, where a purple bruise is blossoming. Her fingers lightly graze over the angry color of the blood collected under my skin.

"Did Sarah give you that?" she asks.

"Yeah," I say, shrugging my bag from one shoulder to another.

"She does that to you a lot," Poppy says, with the borrowed seriousness of an adult. She is nonchalant and yet direct, unwavering as she says this next part: "Friends don't hurt each other."

Poppy's comment is delivered casually, but even as a child, I recognize the weight of what she's saying. I feel intuitively that it's something she's been building up to saying for a while. I press the bruise under my thumb, watching it turn white from the pressure, feeling a sharp pang travel up my arm. Now that Poppy has pointed it out to me, I feel my own pain more acutely; I hear the distant whine of danger approaching, like a siren in the distance.

Throughout the first few months at my new school, I've become used to playing Sarah's "games" at lunch times, which always seem to end with me yelping or flinching in pain. I haven't thought much about it; I've just been grateful to have new friends to spend time with. If a friend is doing something to you, I figured, then it must be friendly—even if what they're doing results in a fist connecting with your arm, your waist, your jaw.

Poppy, through nothing more than an eight-year-old's

instincts and sense of right and wrong, was doing something here that psychotherapists sometimes call "advanced empathy." Advanced empathy is a name for the moment when a therapist hits on something that the client themself has not yet realized or given a name to but which is true for them. But Poppy wasn't peering at me over an analyst's notebook, assessing me with a professional gaze. We were both children, kicking the same pebbles along the street as we dawdled home from school together.

What she was offering me—a noticing, a reflecting of my pain—was a lifeline. She taught me to recognize what hurtful relationships or bullying might look like, and by contrast, what a nurturing and supportive friendship might look like. I learned the difference between a friend who caused me pain, and a friend who saw my pain. However unintentionally, she also showed me how witnessing, acknowledging, and making space for the pain of others is an important step in releasing them from that pain. My continued belief in this principle is no small part of what led me to train as a therapist many years later. It's what I recognize in this memory, and in every story that other people have told me about their experiences of true empathy—that it has the power to release something inside us, to allow us to move toward hope.

At eight years old, as I pressed down on the mark on my forearm, starving it of blood flow and watching it disappear into my skin, I knew intuitively that until Poppy drew my attention to it, I'd been doing exactly that: pressing

Empathy is work

down and avoiding my own pain. Now, thanks to her voicing it, I had permission to feel it and to voice it, too. Her empathy was a breeze cutting through a heatwave. A relief. I lifted my fingers, releasing the pressure from the bruise, and allowed my blood to flow freely back to the places that needed to heal.

Notes

Introduction: Born to read minds?

1. "What is Autism?," NHS, last reviewed September 7, 2022, nhs.uk/conditions/autism/what-is-autism.
2. Uta Frith, *Autism: A Very Short Introduction* (Oxford University Press, 2008), 67; Uta Frith, "Uta Frith: interview," interview by James Rivington, *British Academy Review 28*, The British Academy, June 27, 2016, thebritishacademy.ac.uk/publishing/review/28/uta-frith-interview.
3. Roman Krznaric, *Empathy: Why It Matters, and How to Get It* (TarcherPerigee, 2014), xvi–xvii.
4. "Autism," World Health Organization, November 15, 2023, who.int/news-room/fact-sheets/detail/autism-spectrum-disorders; Rutgers University, "One-fourth of children with autism are undiagnosed," ScienceDaily, January 9, 2020, sciencedaily.com/releases/2020/01/200109130218.htm.
5. *The Good Doctor*, season 1, episode 1, "Burnt Food," directed by Seth Gordon, aired September 25, 2017, on ABC.
6. *The Big Bang Theory*, season 5, episode 24, "The Countdown Reflection," directed by Mark Cendrowski, aired May 10, 2012, on CBS.
7. Hans Asperger, "Die 'Autistischen Psychopathen' im kindesalter," *Archiv für psychiatrie und nervenkrankheiten*, 117, no. 1 (1944): 76–136.

8. Simon Baron-Cohen, *Mindblindness: An Essay on Autism and Theory of Mind* (Bradford Books, 1995).
9. Simon Baron-Cohen, *The Essential Difference: Men, Women and the Extreme Male Brain* (Allen Lane, 2003), 2.
10. "Females and Autism/Aspergers: A Checklist," The Art of Autism, June 10, 2019, the-art-of-autism.com/females-and-aspergers-a-checklist.
11. *The Telepathy Tapes*, hosted and written by Ky Dickens, aired September 9, 2024.
12. Monique Botha et al., "The neurodiversity concept was developed collectively: An overdue correction on the origins of neurodiversity theory," *Autism* 28, no. 6 (2024): 1591–94.
13. Nick Walker, *Neuroqueer Heresies: Notes on the Neurodiversity Paradigm, Autistic Empowerment, and Postnormal Possibilities* (Autonomous Press, 2021).

1. Defining empathy

1. bell hooks, *All About Love: New Visions* (William Morrow Paperbacks, 2000), 4.
2. Connor Nichols, "How Pablo and Unlimited Supported the Met Police's Transformation and Recruitment Drive," *Creative Salon*, July 29, 2024, creative.salon/articles/features/pablo-unlimited-metropolitan-police-change-needs-you-q-a.
3. Sesame Street, "Sesame Street: Mark Ruffalo: Empathy," posted October 14, 2011, YouTube, 02:28, youtube.com/watch?v=9_1Rt1R4xbM&ab_channel=SesameStreet.
4. Harper Lee, *To Kill a Mockingbird* (J. B. Lippincott & Co., 1960), 34.
5. Brené Brown, "The Power of Vulnerability – Brene Brown," posted August 15, 2013, by RSA, YouTube, 21:47, youtube.com/watch?v=sXSjc-pbXk4&t=0s&ab_channel=RSA.
6. Adam Smith, *The Theory of Moral Sentiments* (Penguin Classics, 2009), 22.
7. Joanna Ganczarek et al., "From 'Einfühlung' to empathy: exploring the relationship between aesthetic and interpersonal experience," *Cognitive Processing* 19, no. 2 (2018): 141–45.

Notes

8. Barack Obama, "2006-06-16 - Barack Obama Promotes Empathy: Northwestern Commencement," posted August 26, 2010, by Edwin Rutsch, YouTube, 04:31, youtube.com/watch?v=zEjErLs-Ku8&ab_channel=EdwinRutsch.
9. Rachel Hall, "'Empathy isn't there': the pandemic effects on children's social skills," *The Guardian*, April 4, 2022, theguardian.com/uk-news/2022/apr/04/empathy-isnt-there-the-pandemic-effects-on-childrens-social-skills; Anthony Silard, "The Role of Social Media in Our Empathy Crisis," *Psychology Today*, July 11, 2022, psychologytoday.com/gb/blog/the-art-living-free/202207/the-role-social-media-in-our-empathy-crisis.
10. Elon Musk, "Joe Rogan Experience #2281 – Elon Musk," posted February 28, 2025, by PowerfulJRE, YouTube, 3:11: 07, youtube.com/watch?v=sSOxPJD-VNo&t=4576s&ab_channel=PowerfulJRE.
11. Sigmund Freud, *The Standard Edition of the Complete Psychological Works of Sigmund Freud* (Vintage, 2001), 115.
12. Carl Rogers, *On Becoming a Person: A Therapist's View of Psychotherapy* (Constable, 1961), 34.
13. Carl Rogers, "Empathic: An Unappreciated Way of Being," *The Counseling Psychologist* 5, no. 2 (1975): 2–10.
14. Pete Sanders, *First Steps in Counselling, 2nd edition* (PCCS Books, 1996), 66.
15. Margaret Price, "The Bodymind Problem and the Possibilities of Pain," *Hypatia* 30, no. 1 (2014): 268–84.
16. Paul Bloom, *Against Empathy: The Case for Rational Compassion* (Vintage, 2016).
17. Irvin D. Yalom, *The Gift of Therapy: An Open Letter to a New Generation of Therapists and Their Patients* (Piatkus, 2010), 18.
18. Autistic Self Advocacy Network, *Loud Hands: Autistic People, Speaking* (The Autistic Press, 2012), 17.
19. Hannah Emerson, *The Kissing of Kissing: poems* (Milkweed Editions, 2022), 30.

2. Empathy is humble

1. Catina Burkett, "Autistic while black: How autism amplifies stereotypes," *The Transmitter,* January 21, 2020, thetransmitter.org/spectrum/autistic-while-black-how-autism-amplifies-stereotypes.
2. Simon Baron-Cohen, *Mindblindness: An Essay on Autism and Theory of Mind* (Bradford Books, 1995), 1.
3. Peter Fonagy and Elizabeth Allison, "What is Mentalization? The Concept and Its Foundations in Developmental Research," in *Minding the Child: Mentalization-Based Interventions with Children, Young People and their Families*, ed. N. Midgley and I. Vrouva (Routledge, 2012).
4. Simon Baron-Cohen, *Mindblindness: An Essay on Autism and Theory of Mind* (Bradford Books, 1995).
5. H. V. Soper and M. O. Murray, "Autism," in *The Encyclopedia of Neuropsychological Disorders*, ed. C. A. Noggle, R. S. Dean and A. M. Horton (Springer Publishing, 2012): 125–28.
6. Uta Frith, *Autism: A Very Short Introduction* (Oxford University Press, 2008), 81.
7. Simon Baron-Cohen, *Mindblindness: An Essay on Autism and Theory of Mind* (Bradford Books, 1995), 5.
8. David Premack and Guy Woodruff, "Does the chimpanzee have a theory of mind?," *Behavioral and Brain Sciences* 1, no. 4 (1978): 515–26.
9. Simon Baron-Cohen et al., "Does the autistic child have a 'theory of mind'?," *Cognition* 21, no. 1 (1985): 37–46.
10. Morton Ann Gernsbacher and Melanie Yergeau, "Empirical failures of the claim that autistic people lack a theory of mind," *Archives of Scientific Psychology* 7, no. 1 (2019): 102–18.
11. Simon Baron-Cohen, "The Autistic Child's Theory of Mind: A Case of Specific Developmental Delay," *Journal of Child Psychology and Psychiatry* 30, no. 2 (1989): 285–97.
12. Francesca Happé, "An advanced test of theory of mind: Understanding of story characters' thoughts and feelings by able autistic, mentally handicapped, and normal children and adults," *Journal of Autism and Developmental Disorders* 24 (1994): 129–54.

Notes

13. F. Abell et al., "Do triangles play tricks? Attribution of mental states to animated shapes in normal and abnormal development," *Cognitive Development* 15, no. 1 (2000): 1–16.
14. Simon Baron-Cohen et al., "Reading the Mind in the Eyes Test, RMET," Psychological Testing Online, accessed July 31, 2025, psytests.org/arc/rmeten.html.
15. Carmel Sivaratnam et al., "Brief Report: Assessment of the Social-Emotional Profile in Children with Autism Spectrum Disorders using a Novel Comic Strip Task," *Journal of Autism and Developmental Disorders* 42, no. 11 (2012): 2505–12.
16. Morton Ann Gernsbacher and Melanie Yergeau, "Empirical failures of the claim that autistic people lack a theory of mind," *Archives of Scientific Psychology* 7, no. 1 (2019): 102–18.
17. Alan Costall and Ivan Leudar, "Where is the 'Theory' in Theory of Mind?," *Theory & Psychology* 14, no. 5 (2004): 623–46.
18. Morton Ann Gernsbacher and Jennifer Frymiare, "Does the Autistic Brain Lack Core Modules?," *Journal of Developmental and Learning Disorders* 9 (2005): 3–16.
19. Morton Ann Gernsbacher and Melanie Yergeau, "Empirical failures of the claim that autistic people lack a theory of mind," *Archives of Scientific Psychology* 7, no. 1 (2019): 102–18.
20. Morton Ann Gernsbacher and Jennifer Frymiare, "Does the Autistic Brain Lack Core Modules?," *Journal of Developmental and Learning Disorders* 9 (2005): 3–16.
21. H. Tager-Flusberg and K. Sullivan, "A second look at second-order belief attribution in autism," *Journal of Autism and Developmental Disorders* 24, no. 5 (1994): 577–86.
22. Rachel Cohen-Rottenberg, "A Critique of the Theory of Mind (ToM) Test," Autism and Empathy, accessed July 31, 2025, autismandempathyblog.wordpress.com/a-critique-of-the-theory-of-mind-tom-test.
23. Candida Peterson, "Drawing insight from pictures: the development of concepts of false drawing and false belief in children with deafness, normal hearing, and autism," *Child Development* 73, no. 5 (2002): 1442–59.
24. Alan Costall and Ivan Leudar, "Where is the 'Theory' in Theory of Mind?," *Theory & Psychology* 14, no. 5 (2004): 623–46.

25. Simon Baron-Cohen, *Autism and Asperger Syndrome: The Facts* (Oxford University Press, 2008).
26. Alan Costall and Ivan Leudar, "Where Is the 'Theory' in Theory of Mind?," *Theory & Psychology* 14, no. 5 (2004): 623–46.
27. Melanie Yergeau and Bryce Huebner, "Minding Theory of Mind," *Journal of Social Philosophy* 48, no. 3 (2017): 273–96.
28. Damian Milton, "Embodied sociality and the conditioned relativism of dispositional diversity," *Autonomy, the Critical Journal of Interdisciplinary Autism Studies* 1, no. 3 (2014): 1–7.
29. Damian Milton, "On the ontological status of autism: the 'double empathy problem,'" *Disability & Society* 27, no. 6 (2012): 1–5.
30. Ibid.
31. Rachel Cullen, "The Autistic communication hypothesis: Rachel Cullen educates Annette & Chloe of Aucademy 23.10.2021," streamed on October 23, 2021, by Aucademy, YouTube, 1:48:18, youtube.com/watch?v=qxjTIqrSp-o.
32. David Smukler, "Unauthorized Minds: How 'Theory of Mind' Misrepresents Autism," *Intellectual and Developmental Disabilities* 43, no. 1 (2005): 11–24.
33. "Meltdowns: autistic children and teenagers," Raising Children, last reviewed May 13, 2024, raisingchildren.net.au/autism/behaviour/common-concerns/meltdowns-autistic-children-teenagers; "Autistic Meltdowns and Supporting Your Child," Parent Talk, last reviewed April 2025, parents.actionforchildren.org.uk/development-additional-needs/neurodiversity/autistic-meltdowns.

3. Empathy is embodied

1. Emily Cooke, "Why women aren't from Venus, and men aren't from Mars," *Nature*, November 18, 2022, nature.com/articles/d41586-022-03782-6.
2. Jonathan Chadwick, "Totally addicted to bass! Listening to music triggers the same reward centre in the brain as alcohol and cocaine, study finds," *Daily Mail*, March 29, 2021, dailymail.co.uk/sciencetech/article-9414659/Music-triggers-reward-centre-brain-cocaine-study-finds.html.

Notes

3. Kent C. Berridge and Morten L. Kringelbach, "Pleasure systems in the brain," *Neuron* 86, no. 3 (2015): 646–64.
4. "Know Your Brain: Reward System," Neuroscientifically Challenged, accessed July 31, 2025, neuroscientificallychallenged.com/posts/know-your-brain-reward-system.
5. Ethan S. Bromberg-Martin et al., "Dopamine in motivational control: rewarding, aversive, and alerting," *Neuron* 68, no. 5 (2010): 815–34.
6. Hannah Thomasy, "Debunking the Dopamine Detox Trend," *The Scientist*, July 31, 2024, the-scientist.com/debunking-the-dopamine-detox-trend-72036.
7. David Sander and Lauri Nummenmaa, "Reward and emotion: an affective neuroscience approach," *Current Opinion in Behavioral Sciences* 39 (2021): 161–67.
8. Joseph E. LeDoux, "Coming to terms with fear," *Proceedings of the National Academy of Sciences of the United States of America* 111, no. 8 (2014): 2871–78.
9. "Scientists identify brain's 'anxiety cells'—and how to control them," *New York Post*, February 1, 2018, nypost.com/2018/02/01/scientists-identify-brains-anxiety-cells-and-how-to-control-them; Ryan O'Hare, "Have scientists found the brain's generosity spot? Empathetic people have more activity in a key brain area," *Daily Mail*, August 15, 2016, dailymail.co.uk/sciencetech/article-3741802/Have-scientists-brain-s-generosity-spot-Empathetic-people-activity-key-brain-area.html.
10. Stephanie Preston et al., "Understanding empathy and its disorders through a focus on the neural mechanism," *Cortex* 127 (2020): 347–70.
11. Morton Ann Gernsbacher and Jennifer Frymiare, "Does the Autistic Brain Lack Core Modules?," *Journal of Developmental and Learning Disorders* 9 (2005): 3–16.
12. Chris M. Bird et al., "The impact of extensive medial frontal lobe damage on 'Theory of Mind' and cognition," *Brain* 127, no. 4 (2004): 914–28.
13. Lea Winerman, "The Mind's Mirror," *Monitor on Psychology* 36, no. 9 (2005): 48, apa.org/monitor/oct05/mirror.
14. Ibid.

15. J. H. G. Williams et al., "Imitation, mirror neurons and autism," *Neuroscience and Biobehavioral Reviews* 25, no. 4 (2001): 287–95.
16. Carey Goldberg, "Empathy may begin at the neurons," *The New York Times*, January 10, 2006, nytimes.com/2006/01/10/health/empathy-may-begin-at-the-neurons.html.
17. Gregory Hickok, "Eight Problems for the Mirror Neuron Theory of Action Understanding in Monkeys and Humans," *Journal of Cognitive Neuroscience* 21, no. 7 (2009): 1229–43.
18. Victoria Southgate and Antonia F. de C. Hamilton, "Unbroken mirrors: challenging a theory of Autism," *Trends in Cognitive Sciences* 12, no. 6 (2008): 225–29.
19. Sarah DeWeerdt, "Amygdala, the brain's threat detector, has broad roles in autism," *The Transmitter*, July 14, 2020, thetransmitter.org/spectrum/amygdala-the-brains-threat-detector-has-broad-roles-in-autism.
20. Simon John and Adrian V. Jaeggi, "Oxytocin levels tend to be lower in autistic children: A meta-analysis of 31 studies," *Autism* 25, no. 8 (2021): 2152–61.
21. Teresa Tavassoli et al., "Sensory over-responsivity in adults with autism spectrum conditions," *Autism* 18, no. 4 (2014): 428–32.
22. Simone G. Shamay-Tsoory, "The Neural Bases for Empathy," *The Neuroscientist* 17, no. 1 (2011): 18–24.
23. Francesca Happé and Uta Frith, "Annual Research Review: Towards a developmental neuroscience of atypical social cognition," *Journal of Child Psychology and Psychiatry* 55, no. 6 (2014): 553–57.
24. Anna Machin, "How Men's Bodies Change When They Become Fathers," *The New York Times*, April 15, 2020, nytimes.com/2020/04/15/parenting/baby/fatherhood-mens-bodies.html.
25. Simon Baron-Cohen, *The Essential Difference: Men, Women and the Extreme Male Brain* (Allen Lane, 2003), 1.
26. Ibid, 12.
27. Ibid, 137.
28. "Autistic women and girls," National Autistic Society, accessed August 4, 2025, autism.org.uk/advice-and-guidance/what-is-autism/autistic-women-and-girls.

Notes

29. Simon Baron-Cohen, "The Male Condition," *The New York Times*, August 8, 2005, nytimes.com/2005/08/08/opinion/the-male-condition.html.
30. Jordynn Jack, "'The Extreme Male Brain?' Incrementum and the Rhetorical Gendering of Autism," *Disability Studies Quarterly* 31, no. 3 (2011).
31. Steve Silberman, "The Geek Syndrome," *Wired*, December 1, 2001, wired.com/2001/12/aspergers.
32. Cordelia Fine, *Delusions of Gender: The Real Science Behind Sex Differences* (Icon Books, 2010), xviii.
33. Simon Baron-Cohen, "Delusions of gender—'neurosexism,' biology and politics," *The Psychologist* 23, no. 11 (2010): 904–5.
34. Bonnie Auyeung et al., "Fetal testosterone and autistic traits," *British Journal of Psychology* 100, no. 1 (2009): 1–22, doi.org/10.1348/000712608X311731.
35. Hannah Furfaro, "The extreme male brain, explained," *The Transmitter*, May 1, 2019, thetransmitter.org/spectrum/extreme-male-brain-explained.
36. Karson T. F. Kung et al., "No relationship between prenatal androgen exposure and autistic traits: convergent evidence from studies of children with congenital adrenal hyperplasia and of amniotic testosterone concentrations in typically developing children," *Journal of Child Psychology and Psychiatry* 57, no. 12 (2016): 1455–62.
37. Jessica Wright, "Cognition and behavior: Asperger brains similar across sexes," *The Transmitter*, February 8, 2012, thetransmitter.org/spectrum/cognition-and-behavior-asperger-brains-similar-across-sexes.
38. Jessica Wright, "Brains of women with autism may sport male features," *The Transmitter*, February 23, 2017, thetransmitter.org/spectrum/brains-women-autism-may-sport-male-features.
39. David Greenberg et al., "Testing the Empathizing-Systemizing theory of sex differences and the Extreme Male Brain theory of autism in half a million people," *Proceedings of the National Academy of Sciences of the United States of America* 115, no. 48 (2018): 12152–57.
40. Gina Rippon, *The Gendered Brain: The New Neuroscience that Shatters the Myth of the Female Brain* (The Bodley Head, 2019), 52.

41. David Greenberg et al., "Testing the Empathizing-Systemizing theory of sex differences and the Extreme Male Brain theory of autism in half a million people," *Proceedings of the National Academy of Sciences of the United States of America* 115, no. 48 (2018): 12152–57.
42. Ibid.
43. Sarah DeWeerdt, "Study of nonverbal autism must go beyond words, experts say," *The Transmitter*, September 2, 2013, thetransmitter.org/spectrum/study-of-nonverbal-autism-must-go-beyond-words-experts-say.
44. "Autism," Health and Care of People with Learning Disabilities Experimental Statistics 2020 to 2021, NHS, last edited December 9, 2021, digital.nhs.uk/data-and-information/publications/statistical/health-and-care-of-people-with-learning-disabilities/experimental-statistics-2020-to-2021/autism.
45. Tania Singer and Olga M. Klimecki, "Empathy and compassion," *Current Biology* 24, no. 18 (2014): R875–78.
46. Ibid.
47. Shihui Han, "Neurocognitive Basis of Racial Ingroup Bias in Empathy," *Trends in Cognitive Sciences* 22, no. 5 (2018): 400–21.
48. Hari Srinivasan, "The Myth of the Autism Expert," posted December 26, 2022, by Autistic Neuroscientist, YouTube, 01:04, youtube.com/watch?v=ZJZJ__jt3c4&ab_channel=AutisticNeuroscientist.
49. Kamila Markram and Henry Markram, "The Intense World Theory—a unifying theory of the neurobiology of autism," *Frontiers in Human Neuroscience* 4 (2010): 224.
50. Fern Brady, *Strong Female Character* (Hachette, 2023), 260.
51. Dinah Murray et al., "Attention, monotropism and the diagnostic criteria for autism," *Autism* 9, no. 2 (2005): 139–56.
52. David Robson, "Interoception: the hidden sense that shapes wellbeing," *The Guardian*, August 15, 2021, theguardian.com/science/2021/aug/15/the-hidden-sense-shaping-your-wellbeing-interoception.
53. Emma Goodall, "Interoception and mental wellbeing in autistic people," National Autistic Society, March 16, 2022, autism.org.uk/advice-and-guidance/professional-practice/interoception-wellbeing.
54. "Alexithymia," Autistica, accessed August 4, 2025, autistica.org.uk/what-is-autism/anxiety-and-autism-hub/alexithymia.

55. Geoffrey Bird et al., "Empathic brain responses in insula are modulated by levels of alexithymia but not autism," *Brain* 133, no. 5 (2010): 1515–25.
56. Andrea Putica et al., "Alexithymia in post-traumatic stress disorder is not just emotion numbing: Systematic review of neural evidence and clinical implications," *Journal of Affective Disorders* 278 (2021): 519–27.
57. Savannah Da Silva, "The link between adverse childhood experiences and sensory processing difficulties," The British Psychological Society, January 19, 2024, bps.org.uk/news/link-between-adverse-childhood-experiences-and-sensory-processing-difficulties.
58. Judith Herman, *Trauma and Recovery: The Aftermath of Violence—from Domestic Abuse to Political Terror* (Basic Books, 1992).
59. Stephen W. Porges, "The polyvagal theory: New insights into adaptive reactions of the autonomic nervous system," *Cleveland Clinic Journal of Medicine* 76 suppl. 2 (2009): S86–90.
60. Stephen Porges, "Brain-body connection may ease autistic people's social problems," *The Transmitter*, August 20, 2019, thetransmitter.org/spectrum/brain-body-connection-may-ease-autistic-peoples-social-problems.
61. Caroline Giroux et al., "Polyvagal Approaches: scientifically questionable but useful in practice," *Journal of Psychiatry Reform* 10, no. 11 (2023).

4. Empathy is amoral

1. Paul Bloom, *Against Empathy: The Case for Rational Compassion* (Vintage, 2016).
2. Yiyi Wang et al., "Do Bad People Deserve Empathy? Selective Empathy Based on Targets' Moral Characteristics," *Affective Science* 4, no. 2 (2023): 413–28.
3. Y. Andre Wang and Andrew Todd, "Evaluations of empathizers depend on the target of empathy," *Journal of Personality and Social Psychology* 121, no. 5 (2021): 1005–28.
4. Crystal Raypole, "15 Signs You Might Be an Empath," Healthline, updated July 13, 2023, healthline.com/health/what-is-an-empath.

5. Judith Orloff, "How to Know If You're an Empath," DrJudithOrloff.com, accessed August 4, 2025, drjudithorloff.com/how-to-know-if-youre-an-empath.

6. "Autistic People more likely to feel overwhelming 'hyper-empathy,'" Sheffield Hallam University, February 5, 2024, shu.ac.uk/news/all-articles/latest-news/autism-and-hyper-empathy-study.

7. Marcus Gregory Richardson, "Are You an Empath?," posted January 23, 2024, by marcusgregoryrichardson, TikTok, 05:03, tiktok.com/@marcusgregoryrichardson/video/7327352132275948832?lang=en.

8. Jeffrey Meltzer, "7 Signs You're an Empath," posted May 14, 2024, by Therapytothepoint, TikTok, 01:22, tiktok.com/@therapytothepoint/video/7368634673439804714.

9. Judith Orloff, *The Empath's Survival Guide: Life Strategies for Sensitive People* (Sounds True Adult, 2018), 1.

10. Jia Tolentino, "What Happens When We Decide Everyone Else Is a Narcissist," *The New Yorker*, August 17, 2016, newyorker.com/culture/jia-tolentino/what-happens-when-we-decide-everyone-else-is-a-narcissist.

11. Nadja Heym et al., "The Dark Empath: characterising dark traits in the presence of empathy," *Personality and Individual Differences* 169 (2021).

12. Anita Chaudhuri, "'Narcissists—only more devious': the truth about dark empaths," *The Guardian*, November 10, 2024, theguardian.com/science/2024/nov/10/narcissists-only-more-devious-the-truth-about-dark-empaths.

13. Daisy Jones, "'Dark Empaths' Are Trending. But Should We Be So Quick to Label People?" *British Vogue*, November 12, 2024, vogue.co.uk/article/dark-empath-meaning.

14. Simon Baron-Cohen, *Zero Degrees of Empathy: A New Theory of Human Cruelty and Kindness* (Penguin, 2012), 106.

15. Ibid., 31.

16. Bonnie Rochman, "Guilt by Association: Troubling Legacy of Sandy Hook May Be Backlash Against Children with Autism," *Time*, December 19, 2012, healthland.time.com/2012/12/19/guilt-by-associationtroubling-legacy-of-sandy-hook-may-be-backlash-against-children-with-autism.

Notes

17. "Former Classmate Describes the Adam Lanza He Knew," *PBS News*, December 16, 2012, pbs.org/newshour/education/former-classmate-describes-the-adam-lanza-he-knew.
18. Morénike Giwa Onaiwu, "Don't Let Them Be Autistic...," *Just Being Me... Who Needs "Normalcy" Anyway?*, accessed August 4, 2025, whoneedsnormalcy.com/2014/05/dont-let-them-be-autistic.html.
19. Andrew Solomon, "The Reckoning," *The New Yorker*, March 10, 2014, newyorker.com/magazine/2014/03/17/the-reckoning.
20. Christine Ro, "Autism diagnoses are on the rise—but autism itself may not be," BBC Future, May 10, 2025, bbc.co.uk/future/article/20250509-why-autism-diagnoses-are-on-the-rise.
21. Thomas Mackintosh, "Boy thrown from Tate Modern enjoying swimming lessons," BBC, February 17, 2024, bbc.co.uk/news/uk-england-london-68325469.
22. James W. Kelly and PA Media, "Pride at progress of boy thrown from Tate Modern," BBC, June 10, 2024, bbc.co.uk/news/articles/cp002mr5qyjo; Danyal Hussain, "Boy who was thrown 100 feet from Tate Modern balcony by Jonty Bravery when he was six enjoys first weekend at home and trip to the seaside," *Daily Mail*, August 18, 2020, dailymail.co.uk/news/article-8638269/Boy-thrown-100-feet-Tate-Modern-balcony-Jonty-Bravery-enjoys-weekend-home.html; "Jonty Bravery: Teen who threw boy off Tate Modern jailed as family reveal horrific injuries child is still battling," *Sky News*, June 26, 2020, news.sky.com/story/jonty-bravery-teenager-who-threw-boy-100ft-from-tate-modern-platform-jailed-for-15-years-12015142; "Tate Modern attacker Jonty Bravery had history of violence, report finds," *The Standard*, April 27, 2021, standard.co.uk/news/crime/tate-modern-jonty-bravery-history-violence-report-b932049.html.
23. "Boy who threw six-year-old from Tate Modern was not considered a risk," *The Guardian*, April 27, 2021, web.archive.org/web/20210427143705/theguardian.com/uk-news/2021/apr/27/jonty-bravery-tate-modern-not-considered-risk.
24. "Teenager who threw six-year-old from Tate Modern was not considered a risk," *The Guardian*, April 27, 2021, theguardian.com/uk-news/2021/apr/27/jonty-bravery-tate-modern-not-considered-risk.
25. Ibid.

26. "Tate Modern attack: Jonty Bravery had history of violence, report finds," BBC, April 27, 2021, bbc.co.uk/news/uk-england-london-56881724.
27. Helen Pidd, "Teenagers jailed for 'exceptionally brutal' murder of Brianna Ghey," *The Guardian*, February 2, 2024, theguardian.com/uk-news/2024/feb/02/brianna-ghey-murderers-named-sentenced-to-life-in-prison.
28. Joel Day, "I'm an expert on how serial killers work—this is how I know Lucy Letby is a psychopath," *Express*, August 22, 2023, express.co.uk/news/uk/1804780/lucy-letby-psychopath-serial-killer-expert-spt; Gemma Peplow, "Lucy Letby: Inside the mind of a serial killer—the psychology behind healthcare murderers," *Sky News*, August 19, 2023, news.sky.com/story/lucy-letby-inside-the-mind-of-a-serial-killer-the-psychology-behind-healthcare-murderers-12941902.
29. M. E. Thomas, "'I'm a Psychopath, Here's What Everyone Gets Wrong,'" *Newsweek*, May 9, 2022, newsweek.com/im-psychopath-heres-what-everyone-gets-wrong-1702967.
30. Ellie Broughton, "The big issue: Time to dump the 'dustbin diagnosis'?," British Association of Counselling Professionals, accessed August 4, 2025, bacp.co.uk/bacp-journals/therapy-today/2024/articles-december/the-big-issue.
31. Eli Clare, *Brilliant Imperfection: Grappling with Cure* (Duke University Press, 2017), 41.
32. "The need for abolitionist feminism," Impact/Justice, March 4, 2020, impactjustice.org/need-for-abolitionist-feminism.
33. Sonya C. Faber et al., "The weaponization of medicine: Early psychosis in the Black community and the need for racially informed mental healthcare," *Frontiers in Psychiatry* 9, no. 14 (2023); Rebecca Pinto et al., "Schizophrenia in black Caribbeans living in the UK: an exploration of underlying causes of the high incidence rate," *British Journal of General Practice* 58, no. 551 (2008): 429–34.
34. Louis Favril et al., "Mental and physical health morbidity among people in prisons: an umbrella review," *The Lancet* 9, no. 4 (2024): E250–60.
35. Rollo May, "The Problem of Evil: An Open Letter to Carl Rogers," *Journal of Humanistic Psychology* 22, no. 3 (1982).

Notes

36. "Rollo May Critiques Carl Rogers for Being Naïve About Evil," Passion of Heart, accessed August 4, 2025, passionofheart.co.uk/room-of-no-exit/the-messianic/may-critiques-rogers.

37. Lucy Johnstone, "Do you still need your psychiatric diagnosis? Critiques and alternatives," in *Drop the Disorder!: Challenging the Culture of Psychiatric Diagnosis*, ed. Jo Watson (PCCS Books, 2019).

38. Lucy Johnstone et al., *The Power Threat Meaning Framework: Towards the identification of patterns in emotional distress, unusual experiences and troubled or troubling behaviour, as an alternative to functional psychiatric diagnosis* (British Psychological Society, 2018).

39. C. Daryl Cameron et al., "Empathy Is Hard Work: People Choose to Avoid Empathy Because of Its Cognitive Costs," *Journal of Experimental Psychology* (2019).

40. adrienne maree brown, *Loving Corrections* (AK Press, 2024).

41. Kristin Neff, *Self-Compassion* (Hodder & Stoughton, 2011), 41.

5. Empathy is radical

1. Christophe Maiano, "Prevalence of School Bullying Among Youth with Autism Spectrum Disorders: A Systematic Review and Meta-Analysis," *Autism Research* 9, no. 6 (2016): 601–15.

2. Noah J. Sasson et al., "Neurotypical Peers are Less Willing to Interact with Those with Autism based on Thin Slice Judgments," *Scientific Reports* 7, no. 40700 (2017).

3. Catherine J. Crompton et al., "'I never realised everybody felt as happy as I do when I am around autistic people': A thematic analysis of autistic adults' relationships with autistic and neurotypical friends and family," *Autism* 24, no. 6 (2020): 1438–48.

4. Damian Milton et al., "The 'double empathy problem': Ten years on," *Autism* 26, no. 8 (2022): 1901–3.

5. Catherine J. Crompton et al., "Autistic peer-to-peer information transfer is highly effective," *Autism* 24, no. 7 (2020): 1704–12.

6. Rabi Samil Alkhaldi et al., "Do Neurotypical People Like or Dislike Autistic People?," *Autism in Adulthood* 3, no. 3 (2021): 275–79.

Empathy Takes Action

7. "Autism and BAME?," National Autistic Society, accessed August 4, 2025, autism.org.uk/advice-and-guidance/what-is-autism/autism-and-bame-people.

8. "ASAN Calls for End to Police Violence After Cops Kill Autistic Latino Teen Victor Perez," Autistic Self Advocacy Network, April 14, 2025, autisticadvocacy.org/2025/04/asan-calls-for-end-to-police-violence-after-cops-kill-autistic-latino-teen-victor-perez.

9. Sam Levin, "'A talented, goofy kid': family of Ryan Gainer, autistic teen killed by police, speak out," *The Guardian*, March 22, 2024, theguardian.com/us-news/2024/mar/21/ryan-gainer-autistic-teen-police-killing-california.

10. Said Shaiye, "Black Muslim Autistic Man Walks Thru Airport.docx," accessed August 4, 2025, pitheadchapel.com/black-muslim-autistic.

11. Brené Brown, "Not Looking Away," BreneBrown.com, February 13, 2024, brenebrown.com/articles/2024/02/13/not-looking-away.

12. Brené Brown, "Listening + Learning," BreneBrown.com, February 28, 2024, brenebrown.com/articles/2024/02/28/listening-learning.

13. Hala Alyan, "Why Must Palestinians Audition for Your Empathy?," *The New York Times*, October 25, 2023, nytimes.com/2023/10/25/opinion/palestine-war-empathy.html.

14. "2023–2024 BACP workforce mapping survey," British Association of Counselling Professionals, accessed August 4, 2025, bacp.co.uk/about-us/about-bacp/25-february-2023-2024-bacp-workforce-mapping-survey.

15. "UKCP 2023 Member Survey Report," UK Council for Psychotherapy, accessed August 4, 2025, psychotherapy.org.uk/media/2dfb1l55/2023-ukcp-member-survey-report.pdf.

16. Donna Baines et al., *Doing Anti-Oppressive Practice: Social Justice Work*, 2nd edition (Fernwood, 2011).

17. Marcus Wratten, "Elliot Page wants to combat the 'endless, full-blown lies' about trans lives," *The Pink News*, March 15, 2024, thepinknews.com/2024/03/15/elliot-page-close-to-you-trans-lives.

18. bell hooks, *All About Love: New Visions* (William Morrow Paperbacks, 2000), 221.

Notes

6. Empathy is work

1. Erich Fromm, *The Art of Loving* (Harper & Brothers, 1956), 80.
2. Brad M. Farrant et al., "Empathy, Perspective Taking and Prosocial Behaviour: The Importance of Parenting Practices," *Infant and Child Development* 21, no. 2 (2012): 175–88.
3. Calli Smith and Catherine Stamoulis, "Effects of multidomain environmental and mental health factors on the development of empathetic behaviors and emotions in adolescence," *PLoS ONE* 18, no. 11 (2023).
4. Anne Williford, "The Effect of Bullying and Victimization on Cognitive Empathy Development During the Transition to Middle School," *Child & Youth Care Forum* 45, no. 4 (2016): 525–41.
5. Carl Rogers, *On Becoming a Person: A Therapist's View of Psychotherapy* (Constable, 1961), 16.
6. Matthew J. Bolton, "Decentering Neuronormativity in Humanistic Psychotherapy: Towards a Neurodiversity-Informed, Person-Centered Approach," *The Person-Centered Journal* 26 (2023).
7. Robert Chapman and Monique Botha, "Neurodivergence-informed therapy," *Developmental Medicine & Child Neurology* 65, no. 3 (2023): 310–17.
8. "Autistic Adults' Experiences of Counselling," Autistic Mental Health, accessed August 4, 2025, autisticmentalhealth.uk/counsellingreport.
9. Jennifer Mullan, "Decolonizing Therapy: A Movement—an Interview with Dr. Jennifer Mullan," interview by Curt Widhalm and Katie Vernoy, *Modern Therapist's Survival Guide*, Therapy Reimagined, posted November 6, 2023, therapyreimagined.com/modern-therapist-podcast/decolonizing-therapy-a-movement-an-interview-with-dr-jennifer-mullan.
10. Patty Berne, "Disability Justice—a working draft by Patty Berne," June 10, 2025, static1.squarespace.com/static/5bed3674f8370ad8c02efd9a/t/6329eb83b478e84b6a2502ba/1663691651875/Patty_Berne_DJ-Working-Draft.docx.pdf.
11. Sophie K. Rosa, *Radical Intimacy* (Pluto Press, 2022).

12. "Ethical Framework for the Counselling Professions," British Association of Counselling Professionals, July 1, 2018, bacp.co.uk/events-and-resources/ethics-and-standards/ethical-framework-for-the-counselling-professions.
13. Damon Kirsebom, "Reframing 'Severe' Autism, by Damon Kirsebom," posted November 15, 2020, by Damon Kirsebom, YouTube, 04:56, youtube.com/watch?v=CtK9paFGUjc.
14. Leah Lakshmi Piepzna-Samarasinha, *Care Work: Dreaming Disability Justice* (Arsenal Pulp Press, 2018), 69–73.
15. Ibid.
16. Patty Berne, "Disability Justice—a working draft by Patty Berne," June 10, 2025, static1.squarespace.com/static/5bed3674f8370ad8c02efd9a/t/6329eb83b478e84b6a2502ba/1663691651875/Patty_Berne_DJ-Working-Draft.docx.pdf.

Further Reading

My thinking on empathy has been indelibly shaped by my experiences with disability and illness, through which I've been introduced to the principles of neurodiversity and disability justice.

There are many invaluable resources out there if you'd like to learn more about these topics. The below are some that have been particularly helpful or resonant for me.

All the Weight of Our Dreams: On Living Racialized Autism by Lydia X. Z. Brown et al., eds.

Authoring Autism: On Rhetoric and Neurological Queerness by M. Remi Yergeau

Black Disability Politics by Sami Schalk

Brilliant Imperfection: Grappling with Cure by Eli Clare

The Cancer Journals by Audre Lorde

Care Work: Dreaming Disability Justice by Leah Lakshmi Piepzna-Samarasinha

Disability Intimacy: Essays on Love, Care, and Desire by Alice Wong, ed.

The Emergent Strategy series by adrienne maree brown

Empire of Normality: Neurodiversity and Capitalism by Robert Chapman

Feminist, Queer, Crip by Alison Kafer

Loud Hands: Autistic People, Speaking by the Autistic Self Advocacy Network (ASAN)

Mad World: The Politics of Mental Health by Micha Frazer-Carrol

Neuroqueer Heresies: Notes on the Neurodiversity Paradigm, Autistic Empowerment, and Postnormal Possibilities by Nick Walker

Skin, Tooth, and Bone: The Basis of Movement Is Our People, A Disability Justice Primer by Sins Invalid

Typed Words, Loud Voices by Amy Sequenzia and Elizabeth J. Grace, eds.

Acknowledgments

I am immensely grateful to Milly Reilly, Eva Hodgkin, Sara Zatopek, Bobby Nayyar, Camilla Pang, Freya Alsop, Ally Mitchell, Holly Kyte, Jo Thompson, and Hannah Matuszak and everyone at William Collins, The Experiment, Spread the Word, The Wellcome Collection, Colwill & Peddle, The Society of Authors, and The Authors' Foundation. Thank you to all the interviewees, friends, and supportive colleagues who generously shared their time and thoughts with me both on and off the record during the writing process. Thank you also to everyone who has worked on any aspect of the publication, promotion, and sale of this book.

A special thank you to my early readers, cheerleaders, and support network, who made this work possible: Grace, Salomé, Emily, Evelyn, Louise, Charlie, Alia, Joanna, Jim, Becky, Emma, James, Michele, Adam, Keleisha, Debbie, Ameen (and the whole peer support group), Chris, Sally, and Ruby. And thanks Mum, for reminding me to look at the moon.

About the Author

AIMEE CLIFF is a writer and psychotherapist based in London. She began her career as a music and culture journalist, writing for *The Guardian*, *Pitchfork*, the *FADER*, *Dazed*, and more. In 2021, she won the first iteration of the Wellcome Collection x Spread the Word Writing Awards for her nonfiction book proposal. She currently works as a community counselor and in private practice.

aimeecliff.com